Making
Latino
News

For Max and Rigo, with thanks for everything

América Rodriguez

Making Latino News

Race, Language, Class

Para David,
w/ Thanks for ▌ all your support!
best,
América

Sage Publications, Inc.
International Educational and Professional Publisher
Thousand Oaks ▪ London ▪ New Delhi

Cover photo: The KMEX 6:00 p.m. news team, from left to right: Bernardo Osuna, Andrea Kutyas, and Eduardo Quezada. Copyright © KMEX; used by permission.

For information:

Sage Publications, Inc.
2455 Teller Road
Thousand Oaks, California 91320
E-mail: order@sagepub.com

Sage Publications Ltd.
6 Bonhill Street
London EC2A 4PU
United Kingdom

Sage Publications India Pvt. Ltd.
M-32 Market
Greater Kailash I
New Delhi 110 048 India

Printed in the United States of America

Library of Congress Cataloging-in-Publication Data

Rodriguez, América.
    Making Latino news: Race, language, class / by América
Rodriguez.
    p. cm.
    Includes bibliographical references (p.) and index.

    ISBN 0-7619-1551-6 (paper: alk. paper)
    ISBN 0-7619-1552-4 (cloth: alk. paper)
    1. Hispanic Americans—Press coverage—History. 2.
Journalism—Social aspects—United States. 3. Hispanic American
newspapers—History. 4. Hispanic American mass media—History. 5.
Hispanic Americans and mass media. 6. Hispanic American
journalists. 7. Ethnic press—United States. I. Title.
    PN4888.H57 P63 1999
    070.4'84—ddc21
                                99-6306

99 00 01 02 03 10 9 8 7 6 5 4 3 2 1

Acquiring Editor:	Margaret Seawell
Editorial Assistant:	Renée Piernot
Production Editor:	Diana E. Axelsen
Editorial Assistant:	Patricia Zeman
Typesetters:	Rose Tylak/Tina Hill
Indexer:	Mary Mortensen
Cover Designer:	Candice Harman

Contents

Acknowledgments

Although I accept full responsibility for this work, it has been a collaborative effort. First and foremost, I want to thank the Latino journalists and media professionals who gave me hours of their time: Maria Celeste Arraras, Roxana Boglio, Luis Calle, Milagros Carrasquillo, Berta Castañer, Mayola Delgado, Debbie Durham, Alfredo Estrada, Alina Falcon, Gustavo Godoy, Manny González, Barbara Gutiérrez, Armando Guzman, Ken Hansely, James García, Gustavo Godoy, Christy Haubegger, Alberto Ibarguen, Edwin Jorge, Victor Landa, Lourdes Leahy, Patsy Lorris-Soto, J. Gerardo López, Maria López, Sergio López Miro, Guillermo Martínez, Lourdes Meluzá, Christopher D. Muñoz, Bob Oliva, Valeria Palazio, Gustavo Pompa-Mayo, Eduardo Quezada, Jorge Ramos, Patricia Ramos, Robert Rios, Maria Elena Salinas, Rosalyn Sariol, Javier Sierra, Rafael Tejero, S. Sandra Thomas-Esquivel, Nicolas J. Valls, Robert Vizcon, and Harry Whitman.

I have been fortunate to be taught by superb teachers (thanks, Mom and Dad!)—none more so than Michael Schudson. Many years after my dissertation defense, I often find myself having imaginary conversations with him: "What would Michael think of this?" We don't always agree, but I am invariably enriched by his generous and exacting spirit. Dan Hallin often joins these talks, offering keen insight into political forms and structures.

Mil gracias to Wayne Cornelius, the excellent staff, and the fellows of the Center for U.S.-Mexican Studies of the University of California, San Diego, my first academic home. The center's generous support was financial, intellectual, social, and collegial in ways too many academic institutions don't even attempt, much less exemplify.

In Austin, many thanks to Ellen Wartella, Chuck Whitney, Susan Dirks, John Downing, Nikhil Sinha, Sharon Strover, and Karin Wilkins for their support, friendship, and good cheer. Max Stinchcombe's unstinting research assistance has been invaluable. The University of Texas at Austin, in various guises, provided funding for the field work for this project: the University Research Institute; a Mellon Grant, facilitated by UT's Institute for Latin America Studies (ILAS); a Faculty Research Grant, a subvention grant by the University Cooperative Society, and several smaller grants, all administered by the office of the vice president for research.

The anonymous reviewers of my journal articles, as well as an early version of this book, have sharpened and deepened the analysis. Margaret Seawell, though not physically with me in Austin, has been very much present through the last phases of this project. *Editing* is inadequate to describe the wisdom and perfect pitch she has brought to this work.

Introduction

What Is Latino News?

The production of Latino journalism—news that is purposefully and strategically created for U.S. residents of Latin American descent—symbolically denationalizes Latinos as it renationalizes them as U.S. Hispanics. Latino-oriented news does not melt or displace Latino cultures into the culture of the majority, dominant society, however. Rather, Latino newsmaking creates a detailed symbol system, a daily capsule of reality in which Latinos are seemingly everywhere: among the victims and witnesses of the Oklahoma City bombing, in Congress and city halls, in the professions as well as in the fields and factories. The Latino news world prominently includes Latin America. The making of this social or public knowledge (Hall, 1979, p. 340; Schudson, 1995, p. 3), cultural and economic processes in which issues of power are central, is the topic of this book.

This book is a study of cultural production, of meaning making, by an elite—a Latino elite. Latino journalism is produced by Latino journalists and Latino marketers, Latinos whose cultural and material capital set them apart from much of their intended audience, replicating the social distance that exists between most general market journalists and their audiences. What is, and what isn't, Latino news? These questions are posed of journalism that targets the Latino audience: the national and local television newscasts produced by the principal U.S. Spanish language television networks, *Univisión* and *Telemundo,* the daily Spanish language press (e.g., *La Opinión* and *El Nuevo Herald*), as well as English language and bilingual newspapers and magazines. Latino-oriented media—more than 1,000 broadcast affiliates, including 400 radio stations, hundreds of publications—are one facet of the increasing visibility of the ethnoracial group that will soon be the largest "minority" group in the United States.

By 2020, Latinos will make up about one sixth of all U.S. residents—by 2050, about one quarter (Bureau of the Census, 1997). Put another way, it is predicted that, in less than a generation, one in four people in the United States will be Latino/a. This oft-cited Census Bureau statistic has become a mantra, repeatedly intoned by Latino media producers, Latino marketers, Latino elected officials, and Latino political activists (as well as those who study and teach about Latinos). The evocation of this statistic and its variants—such as, by 2050 the majority of California and Texas populations will be Latino—shouts to the larger, dominant society, "Look at us! You can't ignore us anymore!" The production of Latino news is a social terrain through which Latinos are creating a place for themselves in U.S. culture.

Despite the growth of the Latino population, various studies have documented the symbolic exclusion of Latinos by U.S. general market media.[1] These studies of both entertainment and journalistic media production conclude that in those few instances when Latinos are re-created as members of U.S. society in general market media, they are most often portrayed as criminal or otherwise socially deviant. A pervasive example of the consequences of this representation (and lack of representation) is general market journalism's continuing focus on illegal Latin American immigration to the United States—to the virtual exclusion of other aspects of Latino life.

This preoccupation with illegal immigration has contributed to the misperception that most—or at least many—Latinos are unauthorized immigrants. In fact, undocumented immigrants make up less than 7% of the Latino population, perhaps 3.5 million people (Bureau of the Census, 1997).[2] More than two thirds of U.S. Latinos are U.S. citizens; the rest are is legal residents (Bureau of the Census, 1997). Given this context, Latino politics, including Latino journalism, should properly be considered part of the ongoing U.S. civil rights movement.

The story of U.S. Latino newsmaking is part of another, larger narrative—that of Latin American immigration to the United States. As the following chapters detail, Latino journalism is interwoven into the dynamism of this immigration, and crucially, to the varying receptions Latin American immigrants have received in the United States. As Table 1.1 shows, the largest portion of legal Latin American immigration to the United States has been and is today from Mexico.

Currently nearly two thirds (63%) of Latin American immigration to the United States is from Mexico. A similar proportion of U.S. Latinos is of Mexican heritage (Table 1.2). The first large-scale Cuban immigration to the United States occurred after Fidel Castro's revolution of 1959; a larger number arrived in the 1970s and 1980s, many on homemade rafts. Today, Cubans make up about 4% of Latinos. Also in the 1980s, Central Americans began immigrating in large

Table 1.1. Latin American Immigration to the U.S.[1]

	1901-10	1911-20	1921-30	1931-40	1941-50	1951-60	1961-70	1971-80	1981-90	1991-95
Total[1]	75,114	278,062	533,199	46,704	136,025	525,035	1,115,035	1,4383,673	2,982,391	2,357,215
% of U.S. pop.[2]	0.08	0.26	.43	0.04	0.09	0.29	0.55	0.65	1.20	0.90
Mexico	49,642	219,004	459,287	22,319	60,589	299,811	453,937	640,294	1,655,843	1,490,152
% Total[3]	n/a[4]	n/a[4]	n/a[4]	48	45	57	41	43	56	63
Cuba	n/a[4]	n/a[4]	15,901	9,571	26,313	78,948	208,536	264,863	144,578	65,217
% Total[3]	n/a[4]	n/a[4]	n/a[4]	20	19	15	19	18	5	3
Central America	8,192	17,159	15,796	5,861	21,665	44,751	101,330	134,640	468,088	299,620
% Total[3]	n/a[4]	n/a[4]	n/a[4]	13	16	9	9	9	16	13
South America	17,280	41,899	42,215	7,803	21,831	91,628	257,940	295,741	461,847	283,678
%Total[3]	n/a[4]	n/a[4]	n/a[4]	17	16	17	23	20	15	12

SOURCE: *Statistical Yearbook of the Immigration and Naturalization Service* (1995, Table 2, pp. 28-30).
[1] Immigrants whose last country of residence in the Americas was Spanish speaking (or Brazil).
[2] Latin American immigration divided by U.S. population at end of period.
[3] Immigration from country or region as percentage of total Latin American immigration.
[4] Separate Cuban immigration figures are not available until the mid-1920s.

Table 1.2.   Origin of U.S. Latinos

Mexican	Puerto Rican	Cuban	Central or South American	Other
63%	11%	4%	14%	7%

SOURCE: U.S. Bureau of the Census (1995).

numbers to the United States, fleeing civil wars in El Salvador, Guatemala, and Honduras, and today make up about 14% of U.S. Latinos. Puerto Ricans, the next largest Latino group (about 11% of U.S. Latinos) are not immigrants, and thus are not represented on Table 1.1. Rather, Puerto Ricans became U.S. citizens after the U.S. annexed the island nation early this century.[3] Large-scale Puerto Rican migration from the island to the mainland, principally the New York City metropolitan area, began in the late 1950s and 1960s.

Because of war or economic dislocation (or, most often, a combination of the two), Latin American immigration to the United States has been a continuing feature of the U.S. national story for most of the 20th century. Although Latin America has been the largest source of immigration to the United States this century, only late this century have Latin Americans reached one half of 1% of the U.S. population. The national scope of Tables 1.1 and 1.2 obscures the social force of this immigration on distinct regions of the United States. For instance, Mexican immigrants have largely settled in the southwest states. Similarly, most of the recent Cuban migrants have joined a well-established Cuban American community in south Florida, and 1980s Central American immigrants have largely settled in southern California. At the same time that these geographic concentrations persist, Latinos are increasingly dispersed throughout the country.

As the following chapters detail, Latino journalism has played a central role in maintaining a link between the immigrants and their "home" country, while concurrently these media have been key to the process of adaptation of these immigrants to life in the United States. Today, although new immigrants are a relatively small proportion of Latinos, the importance of Latin America—symbolically and substantively—remains near the center of U.S. Latino newsmaking.

A central theme of this book is membership: cultural, social, and political membership in U.S. society. Historically and today, there has been little room for Latinos (or other non-white peoples) in U.S. civil society. The bifurcation of U.S. race relations into "black and white," as reproduced in general market journalism and many other prominent social institutions, has pushed Latinos to the margins of the U.S. nation. Further, the Latino experience is distinct within U.S. culture because of its transnational character. The most pervasive sign of this is the endurance of the Spanish language and of Spanish language media in the United States. In response to this social landscape, U.S. Latino journalism has carved out an inclusionary role. The Latino journalistic perspectives examined in these pages turn on a vision of Latinos within the national culture, supportive of U.S. society's structures and norms and yet also apart from it, preserving a distinct Latino identity.

Unless otherwise noted, the Latino journalists whose work is cited here are members of what sociologist Ruben Rumbaut (1991) has called the "1.5" or "one and one half" generation, those who were born in Latin America but were educated and came of age in the United States. This "intercultural placement" positions Latino-oriented journalists as translators and mediators between their audience and the dominant, majority society. For Latino journalists, this "in-betweenness" is activated daily in tension between objectivity and ethnicity. Latino journalists are U.S. journalists, trained in traditional U.S. journalism schools, believers and practitioners of the journalistic ideology commonly called "objectivity." At the same time, they are advocates for the inclusion of Latinos in all spheres of U.S. society. This unresolved tension is a defining one for Latino journalists, who are both professional and parochial, committed both to maintaining neutrality and to serving their communities.

The core issue here is the point of view, the vantage point of Latino journalism. This defining perspective is the product of Latino-oriented journalistic firms and their constructions of the presumptive, or targeted, audience. Although this study does not consider audience response to Latino journalism, the journalists' and marketers' conceptualization of the Latino audience is key to the analysis. The creation of a commercially viable Hispanic audience is what makes Latino-oriented journalism possible.

THEORETICAL CONTEXTS

This project fuses cultural and economic analysis. Central to this analysis is the construction of the Latino audience—from a journalistic perspective as well as a marketing or, put another way, commercial culture viewpoint. In this context, the Latino audience is not the men and women who consume news media, but rather the purposeful abstraction that constitutes the economic foundations of Latino journalism—the audience that is bought and sold in the marketplace (Ang, 1991). This audience is a social and cultural and economic construction. The Latino audience is simultaneously the object and the motivator of news production—it is both the purpose and the product of Latino newsmaking. Latino journalism is one of the consequences of Latino audience construction, and Latino journalism is one of the producers of the Latino audience.

This analysis strives not to be media-centric. Rather, news in this volume is contextualized as an element of the societies in which it is produced. Throughout the text, Latino journalism is framed in relation to the institutional and political contexts of its production, as well as the socioeconomic contexts of its intended audiences. The analysis includes, for example, the labor market position of the audiences. In these ways, the production of Latino journalism provides a prism through which to analyze Latino political culture.

Latino-oriented journalists are political actors, and they are actors in the Latino media economy, commonly called the Hispanic market. These two elements of newsmaking are not presented separately, nor as a duality, but as inextricable strands of media production processes (McManus, 1994; Schiller, 1981; Schudson, 1978). Latino journalism is a constitutive element of the social process of community building and identity creation of Latino communities (Carey, 1992; Hall, 1992, 1993). This process of making news by Latino journalists for Latino audiences—the mapping and disseminating of a common social, political, and cultural space, and of an imagined community of shared interests—is an element of the social processes that make up Latino ethnoracial identity.

Ethnicity is a collective identity that arises from daily experience, in the cases examined here, out of the daily experiences of commercial and cultural journalistic production (Hall, 1990; Sánchez, 1993). Similarly, race and racial categorizing are the products of social processes; race is a social construction. Race is one of the hierarchies of U.S. society. The widely disseminated conceptualization of U.S. people of Latin American descent as a unitary race erases the multiracial and multicultural heritage of Latin American societies—both north and south of the U.S.-Mexico border. The racial category *Hispanic* has found a niche in the U.S. ethnoracial stratification *white, black, Hispanic...* The racializing of U.S. communities of Latin American descent—by Latino-oriented media as well as by general market media and the larger society—is a recurring theme of this project (Blauner, 1972; Gandy, 1998; Lipsitz, 1998; Rodríguez, 1989, 1991; Rodríguez & Cordero-Guzman, 1992; Winant, 1994).

The life of the Spanish language in the United States is also key to the analysis. Spanish, in several intersecting contexts of Latino societies, is the preeminent emblem of *Hispanic* in U.S. popular culture. From a nativist point of view, the Spanish language is a sign of "foreignness." From a marketing perspective, the Spanish language is what makes the Hispanic audience "efficient." For many Latino journalists, the Spanish language is an encompassing representation of their audience. The Spanish language as reproduced in Latino newsmaking is, in short, both symbol and substance of Latino ethnoracial identity (Urciuoli, 1996; Woolard, 1985).

Class, in this analysis, is a marker of discrete socioeconomic conditions and, most broadly, of social status or relative social position (Williams, 1983, pp. 60-69). In the case of Latino communities in the United States, class is often conflated with race. An illustration is the response of Latinos to a 1995 U.S. Bureau of Labor Statistics survey. When race and Hispanic origin questions were asked separately, 95% of Cuban Americans—the Latino group with the highest median family income—identified themselves as white. In sharp contrast, more than a third of the Mexican American and Puerto Rican respondents racially identified themselves as multiracial or other. Representations of class in Latino newsmaking are, in most U.S. journalism, far from explicit. Nonetheless, and again like the general media market, hierarchical class distinctions are central to Latino media "audience making."

The production of the Hispanic audience and Latino newsmaking have, from the 19th century to the present, been part of the globalization of communication, of the transnational production of culture. This project's focus is on how structural and cultural globalizing forces are manifest in U.S. Latino national and local commercial cultures, particularly as regards the "spacialization" (Mosco, 1996) of Latino journalism as a segment of a Latin America centered "cultural-linguistic market" (Wilkinson, 1995). This analysis is mindful that transnationalization of culture does not necessarily entail the homogenization or the obliteration of national cultures (Martin Barbero, 1987; Morley & Robbins, 1995; Sinclair, 1996).

Latino newsmaking and conceptualizations of Latino race, language, and class are evolving social, political, and cultural processes. One of the goals of this project has been to complicate Latino namings and categorizations, rejecting what Stuart Hall calls the "essentializing" of identities. For example, while acknowledging the power of the "Hispanic market," the study also highlights the social and cultural distinctiveness of national origin identified Latino groups such as Mexican Americans, Cuban Americans, and Puerto Ricans. The analysis that follows recognizes that Latino audiences, and the news media produced for them, have internal differences that are not erased by unitary ethnoracial labeling.

Making Latino News: Race, Language, Class draws on 42 open-ended interviews with Latino journalists, audience researchers, and marketers in New York, Washington, D.C., Chicago, Los Angeles, and San Antonio. Unless otherwise noted, these interviews were conducted in person and in English by me. Also, I conducted content and textual analysis of select Latino news media texts and Hispanic market research reports.

Part I provides the historical and commercial contexts of Latino-oriented news production. Chapter 2 examines U.S. Spanish language newspapers of the late 19th and early 20th centuries, highlighting their role in the developing political culture of Mexican Americans in the southwestern United States. The chapter profiles several U.S. Spanish language newspapers of the period following the treaty of 1848, with which the U.S. annexed half of Mexico (see Figure 2.1), and of the Mexican Revolutionary era in the early decades of the 20th century. The genesis of U.S. Spanish language media institutions is interwoven with other key points in Mexican American social history: large-scale immigration from Mexico to the southwestern United States, the massive deportations of the 1930s and 1950s, and the beginnings of Mexican American participation in the U.S. electoral arena.

Chapter 3 shifts the analytical focus to the development of what is today called the "Hispanic audience," the nexus of the Hispanic consumer market, the bedrock of contemporary Latino media. This approach facilitates an examination of the historical evolution of U.S. Spanish language broadcasting. These media embody the close relation between Mexican media and media located north of the Rio Grande, or as Mexicans call this border river, *el Rio Bravo.*

Chapter 4 chronologically examines the cultural and commercial production of the contemporary Hispanic audience and contemporary Latino-oriented media institutions. Included here is an analysis of the development of the National Hispanic Television Index and the work of other Hispanic audience researchers and marketers, work that has transformed U.S. residents of Latin American descent into a viable commercial product.

Part II analyzes the production of different spheres of Latino news, examining how Latino news is made, as well as how and why Latino news workers do this particular kind of newsmaking. At the center of the answers to these queries is the conceptualizations that journalists have of their audiences.

Chapter 5 examines the production of news for the U.S. nation of Latinos, focusing specifically on the most widely distributed of these national journalistic productions, the Spanish-language television programs *Noticiero Univisión,* and the U.S. edition of CBS-*Telenoticias.* U.S. Latino news constructs and promotes U.S. nationalism as it creates a symbolic space for Latinos within the United States. National Latino newsmaking turns on the notion that people of Latin American descent who reside in the United States are full members of U.S. society, deserving of equitable treatment. This chapter also includes a consideration of these national newscasts' coverage of Latin America.

Chapter 6 discusses local U.S. Latino news, in particular news that is produced for the Latinos of Los Angeles and Miami. This examination offers a window on the diversity of Latino communities and the journalism that is produced for them. English-language and bilingual Latino journalism is the newest and least institutionalized form of Latino newsmaking. Chapter 7 analyzes the content and the target audiences of these emergent Latino media. Chapter 8 concludes the study with a discussion of the future of Latino newsmaking.

NOTES

1. An excellent summary is a report by Navarrete and Kamasaki (1994). See also Berg (1990); Ericksen (1981); Gerbner (1993); Greenberg and Brand (1994); Keever,

Martindale, and Weston (1997); Lichter and Lichter (1988); Lichter, Lichter, and Rothman (1991); Martindale (1995); Morales (1996); *News Brownout* (National Council of La Raza, 1998); and Subervi Vélez (1994).

2. Most undocumented immigrants do not creep into the United States under cover of darkness, but are, as the Immigration and Naturalization Service (INS) calls them, "overstays." That is, they are people who enter the United States legally, say on a tourist, business, or student visa, and then remain in the United States after the visa has expired (Bean, Edmonston, & Passel, 1990; see also Bean & Tienda, 1987, pp. 117-121).

3. The United States took control of Puerto Rico following its victory in the Spanish American War in 1898. In 1917, the U.S. Congress passed the Jones Act, declaring Puerto Ricans U.S. Citizens.

PART I

History and Context

Cultural identities come from somewhere, have histories. But like every-thing that is historical, they undergo constant transformation. Far from be-ing eternally fixed in some essentialist past, they are subject to the continu-ous "play" of history, culture and power. Far from being grounded in the mere "recovery" of the past . . . identities are the names we give to the differ-ent ways we are positioned by, and position ourselves within, the narratives of the past. (Hall, 1990, p. 224)

The next three chapters offer a historical framing of the cultural, commercial, and political processes that are the making of Latino news. Three principal threads run through Latino journalism over time and across media. One is that of cultural resistance to the dominant culture. The second, closely related, thread is that of cultural preservation, or put another way, the re-creation of Latin Ameri-can cultural forms in the United States. Early U.S. Spanish language newspa-pers' and broadcast programs' maintenance of Mexican culture in the United States, for example, had an economic component: the need to attract an audience and so to survive in the marketplace. Another thread is that of accommodation to the dominant society. This last facet of the history of Latino media production includes political and cultural integration into the dominant U.S. society, as well as the attempted inclusion of these media into the commercial media sphere. This history is paradoxical, never neatly contradictory.

U.S. Spanish Language Newspapers
1848-1970

As shown in Figure 2.1, about 150 years—roughly five generations—ago the southwestern United States was Mexico. From another point of view, about half of what was Mexico in 1848 is today the United States. Thus, in the context of the history of the U.S. "immigrant press," early Latino media are somewhat anomalous. Unlike the dominant U.S. immigrant story of Western European migration to the United States, the Mexican American (like the African American) founding story is not one of optimistic passage, but of bloody conquest. With the end of the Mexican War and the signing of the Treaty of Guadeloupe Hidalgo in 1848, the United States annexed half of Mexico, a territory that includes the states of California, Nevada, Utah, Arizona, New Mexico, and Texas, and parts of Colorado and Kansas.

The Mexicans living in these territories, although granted nominal U.S. citizenship by the treaty, were socially, politically, and culturally stranded, becoming aliens in their own land. Unlike European immigrants to the United States, Mexicans did not choose to be immigrants; the treaty of 1848 made them immigrants in the land of their birth.[1] Echoes of the resultant feelings of displacement and alienation, of being treated as a stranger in one's own home, are still heard today in Mexican American culture, including news media production.

This chapter examines the early decades of U.S. Spanish language newspapers, focusing on the evolution of the often highly politicized content of these media and the social context that shaped them. This discussion of 19th- and early 20th-century newspapers foregrounds these media's construction of their

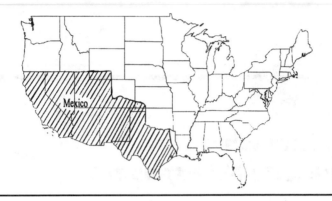

Figure 2.1. United States, 1830

audience's political and cultural identity. Key to understanding these examples of early Latino media is an appreciation of the porousness of the U.S.-Mexican border and the isolation of Mexican and Mexican American society from that of the larger Anglo or European American society.

The first Latino news media were not newspapers, but an oral cultural form, *corridos,* the "musical press" (Cortes, 1987). *Corridos,* topical ballads that originated in the U.S.-Texas borderlands in the mid-19th century, were "generated by the stark social oppositions of the border region, a response to differential—not shared—identity . . . The generating force out of which such folklore emerges is conflict, struggle, and resistance" (Bauman, 1993, p. xiv).

Perhaps the best known of the *corridos* is the "Ballad of Gregorio Cortez," the story of a Mexican American man wrongfully persecuted by the Texas Rangers, the state's military arm. The heroic ballad, highly textured with specific historical detail, is a retelling of history from the point of view of the newly dispossessed and disenfranchised peoples of the Rio Grande Valley (Paredes, 1958). The counter-hegemonic stance inaugurated in the *corridos,* although often muted, is a continuing feature of Latino news.

Late 19th- and early 20th-century U.S. Spanish language newspapers, most weekly or semiweekly and short lived, were among the very first civil society institutions created by Mexicans and Mexican Americans in the southwestern United States. Hundreds have been documented by historians (see Gutiérrez, 1977). As the examples discussed below show, these newspapers are diverse in their political stances and content. They share defining characteristics, however. They were the public voice of Mexicans and Mexican Americans; they defended the interests of these often-embattled peoples as they helped create a common culture for their communities.

Whether the U.S. government, fraternal organizations, or local businesses, the economic structures that supported these newspapers were elements of a nascent Mexican American consumer economy—an economic system that was largely marginalized within the larger society. For example, *casas de cambio,* or money exchanges, were principal advertisers in the Spanish language press in the 19th century (as they are today). Typically housed in the segregated *barrio,* or Latino neighborhood, the money exchanges cater to particular needs of immigrants—to change foreign money to U.S. dollars, and to send money to another country—a consumer practice not commonly found in Anglo society. Similarly, ethnic bakeries, immigration lawyers, and Spanish language newspapers are created for a distinct, usually socially separate, category of consumer.

LATE 19TH-CENTURY NEWSPAPERS

After 1848, the first newspapers produced by and for Mexicans and Mexican Americans in the newly conquered territories were subsidized by the state of California as a part of the "domestic cycle of conquest . . . [and] internal colonization" (Gutiérrez, 1977, p. 37).[2] Also during this period, privately owned general market newspapers in Texas, New Mexico, and Arizona offered Spanish language sections. The Mexican journalists employed by these newspapers were largely translators. Their accommodationist stance foreshadowed later intraethnic political and class tensions; they were considered "establishment Mexicans." In 1879, Tucson's *El Fronterizo* reprinted an article from the *Arizona Citizen* complimenting the Spanish language newspaper on its role as "the organ of good Mexicans" (Gutiérrez, 1977, pp. 38-39).

In contrast, *El Clamor Público* (the Public Clamor, or Shouting), though partially subsidized by the government of Los Angeles, saw itself as an organ of activist resistance to the state. This passage is from a June 1858 editorial:

> The North Americans pretend to give us lessons in humanity and to bring our people the doctrine of salvation so we can govern ourselves, to respect the laws and conserve order. Are these the ones who treat us worse than slaves? (Gutiérrez, 1977, pp. 40)

El Clamor Público closed in 1859 because of insufficient funds, but across the southwest, dozens of Spanish language newspapers were formed in this period.[3] Most of these newspapers exposed atrocities and demanded public services, all the while urging their readers to fight back against European American mistreatment of Mexicans in the United States.

EARLY 20TH-CENTURY NEWSPAPERS

Between 1900 and 1930, more than 1 million Mexicans crossed the border, fleeing the Mexican Revolution (see Table 1.1). This "immigrant generation"
(García, 1989) thought of itself as *México de afuera,* the Mexico of the outside.
The U.S. Spanish language press of this period, although not completely abandoning the activist stance of the previous decades, was preoccupied with the
war, and featured more news of Mexico than of the United States. The largest
concentration of Mexican immigrants in this period settled in the Los Angeles
area and were manual laborers. These mainly railroad and agricultural workers,
many transported from Mexico in boxcars, provided the backbone of the economic expansion of the southwestern United States.

The largest of the Los Angeles Spanish language newspapers (circulation
4,000) was *El Heraldo de México* (1916-1920), which billed itself as the "Defender of Mexicans in the United States." Its primary mission was combating
discrimination and exploitation of Mexican immigrants. The newspaper organized a protective league for immigrant workers. Headlines such as "The Exploit-
ers Beware! Mexicans Beware!" illustrate calls for collective action, as do testimonials such as this one:

> Excuse the molestation I bring in the name of more than 30 Mexicans who find our-
> selves here in the desert . . . They brought us with the hoax that we were going to
> camp at Salt Lake . . . A number of comrades have died on the road. The contractors
> promised us a wage of $1.75 daily, but it is a lie . . . Do me a favor and publish these
> words . . . so that they serve as a warning to other fellow countrymen: [that they]
> not allow themselves to be tricked. (Chacón, 1977, p. 62)

El Heraldo, published by businessman Cesar Marburg, regularly ran advertisements from employers from throughout the southwest who were looking for laborers.

The Mexican Revolution (1910-1917) provided the "push factor" for this
wave of immigration. It was, according to several historians (see, e.g., Acuña,
1988), launched in the U.S. barrios of San Antonio, Laredo, El Paso, and Los
Angeles. Revolutionary factional leaders directed the war from the U.S. side of
the border, publicizing their views and raising funds. Several U.S. Spanish language newspapers were clearly identified with various revolutionary factions.
These newspapers' editors (like their U.S. border region English language counterparts) sometimes changed their alliances over the course of the war, responding to pressure from both the Mexican and, later, the U.S. government. After
1913, many of these newspapers began to question continuation of the violence,
with most speaking out against threatened U.S. intervention. Many ran adver-

tisements selling armaments and soliciting U.S. residents to join rebel armies, thereby risking a violation of the U.S. neutrality laws (Griswold del Castillo, 1977).

Los Angeles's *Regeneración* and other working-class-oriented Spanish language newspapers were also concerned with relating the war's bloodshed to the lives of Mexican immigrants in the United States. These newspapers drew parallels between the corruption of some Mexican public officials and that of some European American politicians in the United States. Perhaps the most important consequence of the Mexican Revolution for Mexican Americans, and their press, was

> the heightening of feelings of nationalism and love of *la patria* (the homeland, Mexico) . . . The Mexican Revolution . . . had a far reaching impact on the Spanish speaking society in the United States, increasing their numbers through immigration and reinforcing their ties and loyalties to Mexico . . . The Mexican American editors had helped give birth to this emerging sense of nationalism—a force that would have lasting consequences on both sides of the border. (Griswold del Castillo, 1977, pp. 43-47)

LA PRENSA OF SAN ANTONIO (1913-1957)

In contrast to the Los Angeles immigrant working-class newspapers discussed above, San Antonio's *La Prensa* was a middle-class Mexican *exile* newspaper written by and for the small percentage of educated Mexican immigrants of the period.[4] *La Prensa*'s ownership, presumptive early audience, and content represented another facet of Mexican immigration to the United States that resulted from the Mexican Revolution, that of the privileged and educated. This editorial stance would change somewhat over time. Remaining constant throughout its history, however, was *La Prensa*'s commitment to being a profitable Mexican American enterprise.

When Mexican-born Ignacio Lozano founded *La Prensa* in 1913 as a weekly newspaper, the Mexican Revolution was raging. Lozano had some literary journalism experience in Mexico and entrepreneurial ambitions. In addition to *La Prensa*, Lozano created a book publishing company, the *Editorial Lozano*. Politically, Lozano and *La Prensa* consistently took the position that Mexico would be better off returning to the prerevolutionary era of the *Porfiriato*, the late 19th-century period named for the dictator and Europhile Porfirio Diaz. Lozano and his newspaper, committed to the cultural education of their readers, each Sunday published European literature, the (translated) writings of such authors as Guy de Maupassant, Honoré de Balzac, Tolstoy, and George Bernard Shaw.

Above all else, Lozano considered himself a Mexican patriot. *La Prensa* was dominated by Mexican news and was a haven for exiled Mexican literary and political authors. This editorial policy was an immediate commercial success. *La Prensa*'s circulation after its first year was 10,000. A year later, it began daily publication, and circulation doubled. It was read throughout south, central, and west Texas; this regional circulation, partially delivered by mail, crossed the border and extended into northern Mexico. "Lozano had discovered that a good percentage of the native population of . . . Texas, even some who had never been to Mexico, wanted to be Mexican and considered themselves Mexican, perhaps because the Anglo American kept telling them exactly that" (Novoa, 1989, p. 151).

La Prensa's presumptive readers were Mexicans whose self-concept was that of an exile, not an immigrant-people waiting for an opportunity to return home, never relinquishing or displacing this primary identity with a U.S. one. Through detailed and continuing coverage of Mexican politics, as well as Mexican arts and letters, *La Prensa* kept its readers in touch with the homeland, nurturing a sense of community. The fulcrum of that commonality was Mexico.

Beginning in 1915, *La Prensa* annually published a 40-page special edition on September 15, Mexican independence (from Spain) day. *La Prensa* and its editor/publisher also took on the role of community leader, sponsoring San Antonio commemorations of other Mexican national holidays, community *fiestas* (festivals), and fund raisers for victims of natural disasters, both in Texas and in Mexico. At one of these events, Lozano proclaimed,

> The day shall come no doubt when all of us are restored to the loving arms of our homeland. . . . Until that day arrives, you, workman, continue operating that machine . . . When we have the good fortune to return to our homeland . . . we shall see a Mexican sun that illuminates the last twilight of our life. (as cited in Rios-McMillan, 1989, p. 141)

Lozano never returned to Mexico, nor did his family. Although never abandoning the nostalgic vision of Mexico or daily continuing coverage of Mexican politics, *La Prensa*'s content by the end of its first decade reflected a shift of the newspaper's focus to this side of the border, or as many Mexican Americans still say today, *"acá, el México de este lado,"* over here, the Mexico of this side.

La Prensa took on the role of protecting Mexican children in the United States from discrimination in the public schools. Instead of the confrontational editorials and organizing efforts of the working-class newspapers, *La Prensa* urged calm study of the issues and rational discussion. Similarly, the newspaper cautioned newly arriving unauthorized Mexican immigrants to be aware of *enganchadores,* immigrant smugglers today known as "coyotes," urging them to educate themselves and work hard, encouraging middle-class aspirations. In addition, *La Prensa* began covering Hollywood and U.S. sports, running advice columns for U.S. farmer, and translating U.S. literary works. Reverence for and identification with Mexico, however, was never far from *La Prensa*'s core identity.

During the Great Depression, between 1929 and 1939, 500,000 to 600,000 Mexicans (including many U.S. citizens) were deported from the United States. Some Mexicans and Mexican Americans wanted to go, and their return to Mexico was facilitated by private and governmental social workers. A larger number of deportations, especially in Texas, were forced, a continuation of the violence between Mexicans and vigilante Anglo groups that had existed since the middle of the previous century (Acuña, 1988, pp. 198-244).

During this period, *La Prensa* remained nonconfrontational and optimistic, supporting the Mexican government's department of repatriation, which promised work camps in Mexico for the deportees. Cooperating with Mexican consulates, *La Prensa* disseminated information about the camps in several Texas cities. The Mexican government underestimated the number of people who wanted to return home, and the camps soon collapsed.

La Prensa suffered during the depression: Its readership base was eroded by deportations, and many of its advertisers were financially ruined. By the late thirties, however, the newspaper, with permanent correspondents in Paris and Washington, D.C., had rebounded. Lozano had diversified, and so protected himself, before the depression. Following the bulk of new Mexican immigration to California, in 1926 he founded a Los Angeles daily, *La Opinión,* and moved most of his companies' assets west.

The depression years also signaled a further change in Lozano's political philosophy. Although *La Prensa* continued to sponsor patriotic Mexican functions, it no longer downplayed the permanence of Mexicans in the United States. Most notably, *La Prensa* increased its attention to Mexican American political representation in the United States, especially after the return of Mexican American soldiers from World War II. In the 1950s, *La Prensa* influenced various local San Antonio and central Texas elections, including the election of state senator Henry B. González, the future congressman, son of the longtime managing editor of *La Prensa.*[5]

The last edition of *La Prensa* was published in 1957. The Lozano enterprise continues to thrive today, however, with *La Prensa*'s Los Angeles sister newspaper, *La Opinión.*

IGNACIO LÓPEZ AND *EL ESPECTADOR* (1933-1961)

Ignacio López, the publisher, editor, and chief reporter of *El Espectador,* a Spanish language weekly published in the San Gabriel Valley (east of Los Angeles), is an exemplar of what historian Mario García calls the "Mexican American generation," community leaders who between 1930 and 1960 initiated the struggle for Mexican American civil rights.[6] Beginning in 1930 (and continuing today), the majority of "Mexicans" in the United States were born and raised in the United States. No longer immigrants, yet clearly members of a marginalized group, "they hungrily pursued the American Dream . . . [and] the development of community and ethnic consciousness: Mexican-Americanism" (García, 1989, pp. 16, 20). In contrast to the 19th- and early 20th-century journalists discussed above, López recognized and encouraged the permanency of the Mexican American community in the United States. Through *El Espectador,* he promoted the political and cultural integration of Mexican Americans into the larger society.

López conceived of his journalistic role as one of community leadership and advocacy for what he perceived to be the interests of the Mexican American community. His opinions were expressed in the pages of *El Espectador* and in numerous negotiations he held with Anglo community leaders and public officials. Examples of these include boycotts López and his newspaper organized against area movie theaters, bars, and public swimming pools, as well as a cemetery, all of which segregated their Mexican American customers.

López also spearheaded public campaigns against police brutality against Mexicans and Mexican Americans, as well as efforts to desegregate public housing and public schools. Throughout this political activism, López chastised the Mexican American community, trying to shake it out of what López called its "lethargy." Throughout the 1930s and 1940s, *El Espectador* editorials often featured sentences like this one: "The only ones to blame for the insults perpetrated against us are ourselves" (García, 1989, p. 88). López's refusal or inability to recognize structured, institutional racism was rooted in his faith in the U.S. political system, the equal rights of all its citizens, and the future of U.S. cultural pluralism.

López did not believe in, or advocate assimilation, however, the complete absorption of Mexican American culture into that of Anglo society, the process represented by the metaphor of the melting pot. Rather, *El Espectador*'s editorial page contained these words:

> The beauty and the strength of our America lies not in being alike, but in our differences . . . Continue united, for unity builds strength and continue to be proud of being born in the United States and of having Mexican blood in your veins. (García, 1989, p. 106)

Supporting this notion of biculturalism, *El Espectador* regularly organized celebrations of Mexican patriotic holidays and ran a series called *¿Conoce Usted México?* (Do You Know Mexico?) about the history of prominent Mexican institutions. At the same time, a weekly column, *Sus Derechos* (Your Rights), was written by a Mexican American attorney.

After World War II and the return home of Mexican American veterans, López redoubled his voter registration efforts, writing, "The vote is our most sacred right and at the same time, our most powerful political weapon" (García, 1989, p. 101). With the help of a political organization López helped found, several Mexican Americans were elected to office in the San Gabriel Valley. One advertisement that ran in *El Espectador* proclaimed, "Elect one of your own, who feels and understands your needs and problems" (García, 1989, p. 103).

In time, López qualified his support for ethnic politics, and he became active in national politics. In 1961, he closed *El Espectador* for financial reasons. He worked on Richard Nixon's presidential campaigns; in 1972, he was rewarded with an undersecretary position with the Department of Housing and Urban Development.

LA OPINIÓN

La Opinión, which is published today, is the longest running, continuously published Spanish language daily newspaper in the United States.[7] An examination of its early years shows the interaction of commercial acumen and cultural tenacity as the source of its resiliency.

In the 1920s, Los Angeles surpassed San Antonio as the U.S. city with the largest concentration of Mexicans. Ignacio Lozano noticed that *La Prensa,* published hundreds of miles away in San Antonio, Texas, was in great demand in California; his decision to open another Spanish language daily newspaper in Los Angeles in 1926 was, in large part, a marketing decision. By its second year of publication, *La Opinión,* which reprinted some of the same editorials (and news stories) as *La Prensa,* was turning a profit. It was distributed in Texas, New Mexico, Oregon, Kansas, Arizona, Utah, and Illinois, in addition to California (Medeiros, 1980, p. 68).

The commercial success of *La Opinión* (and many other newspapers of the period, both Spanish and English language) was made possible by the increasing urbanization of the United States—the beginnings of the shift of much of the U.S. population from the countryside and agricultural work to the cities and industrial labor, including menial, service sector, and professional occupations. The transformation of the U.S. labor force was differentiated by race. In 1917, 91.5% of Mexicans in Los Angeles worked in blue-collar jobs, in contrast to just over 50% of Anglos. Seven out of ten Mexicans performed menial labor, compared to 6% of white Anglos (Romo, 1983, p. 102). Mexican job safety, housing, education, and health conditions were often appalling.

Francine Medeiros's (1980) content analysis of *La Opinión* from 1926 to 1928 shows that although the newspaper was critical of the abuses of Mexicans by the dominant society, overall it gave little coverage to Mexicans in the United States: 10.6% of the editorials and 11.5% of the newspaper's headlines were about Mexicans in the United States; the great majority of the rest of *La Opinión* was about Mexico, with the remainder about other international news. Of the coverage of Mexicans in the United States, about a fourth (25.4%) of the editorials were about the problems of the immigrants. These were about "cultural preservation and the dangers of assimilation and acculturation . . . Lozano deemed resistance to Americanization as the heaviest burden shouldered by Mexicans in the U.S." (pp. 70, 75). This editorial stance was consistent with the position Lozano took in his San Antonio newspaper, *La Prensa*: Mexicans were in the United States only temporarily, until conditions improved in Mexico.

The second-largest category of editorials about Mexicans in the United States was pleas "not to behave according to the racist beliefs of a white society: dirty, lazy, disease ridden, ignorant" (Medeiros, 1980, p. 80). Although *La Opinión* editorialized against negative stereotypes and recognized that they were the creation of Anglo society, it placed the responsibility for destroying the stereotypes on the Mexican community. Accordingly, the newspaper also wrote positive stories about the Los Angeles Mexican community, holding up good students and hardworking laborers for emulation. At the same time, *La Opinión* editorialized in support of Mexican women garment worker strikes and facilitated the created of *mutualistas,* worker protection leagues (Sánchez, 1993, p. 238).

When forced deportations began in the 1930s, the Los Angeles Spanish language daily reported on the beatings of Mexicans by the Los Angeles Police Department (LAPD), as well as LAPD raids and arrests. The *Los Angeles Times* generally did not report on the deportation abuses of Mexicans and Mexican Americans in Los Angeles. This excerpt from a 1933 *Los Angeles Times* story about the meaning of the deportations illustrates the stark difference in the points of view of the two Los Angeles dailies: "The exodus saved the taxpayers about $2,000,000 that otherwise would have been spent caring for these destitute Mexicans" (Chavira, 1977, p. 60).

During the 1954 deportations, dubbed "Operation Wetback" by the Immigration and Naturalization Service (INS), *La Opinión* carried stories about a "concentration camp" in a city park, innocent people swept up in raids, and public protests against the state action against Mexicans and Mexican Americans. The *Los Angeles Times* did not report these events (Chavira, 1977).

Like *La Prensa* and *El Espectador,* *La Opinión* took a leading role in the attempted integration of the Los Angeles Mexican American community in electoral politics. With its sponsorship and editorial endorsement of voter registration drives and the formation of such middle-class Mexican American political groups as the League of United Latin American Citizens (LULAC) and the GI

Forum, *La Opinión* supported the ethnic politics that led to the election of Congressman Ed Roybal and other Mexican American officials in the postwar years.

In 1959, the *Los Angeles Times* hired Rubén Salazar, a Mexican American journalist, as a reporter. He covered Central America, Mexico, and the border region, and then did a tour of duty for the *Times* in Vietnam. Once back in Los Angeles, Salazar's beat was the growing Mexican American community. In the spring of 1970, Salazar left the *Times* to become news director for Spanish language television station KMEX-TV, the Los Angeles affiliate of the Spanish International Network, SIN.

Salazar's shooting death in August 1970 during the Chicano Moratorium, a massive antiwar and civil rights demonstration, made him a martyr and a hero for Chicanos. Days of largely nonviolent protests ended violently—two other people besides Salazar died, 61 were injured, and there was widespread property damage in East Los Angeles, a predominantly Mexican American neighborhood. Photographers for *La Raza* (The Race), a Spanish language magazine, documented police misconduct (the photographs were published in both *La Raza* and the *Los Angeles Times*). After a 16-day inquest televised on KMEX-TV, it was determined that Salazar was killed by a sheriff's projectile, but no one was prosecuted for the journalist's death (Acuña, 1988, pp. 345-350; García, 1995).

At both the *Times* and KMEX, Salazar wrote about issues of Chicano identity and civil rights, including mistreatment by the police. For the *Times,*

> Salazar represented a responsible and professional voice or "translator" that the *Times* could accommodate; at the same time, his voice could be utilized as a way for the Chicano movement to communicate with and to challenge the establishment, a paradoxical role not uncommon for minority professionals. (García, 1995, p. 30)

Salazar took up his position at Los Angeles's Spanish language television station because, he said, "I really wanted to communicate with the people I had written so much about." And yet, an associate remembers how furious Salazar once became when someone referred to him as a "Chicano newsman": "I'm a newsman. I'm a journalist who happens to be Chicano. Don't you ever call me a Chicano newsman" (García, 1995, pp. 30, 34). The tension in Salazar's comments between loyalty to his community and professional journalistic standards foreshadowed tensions experienced by contemporary Latino journalists.

In this period of racial unrest, political assassinations, and societal upheaval, *La Opinión* journalists created a front page emblematic of Mexican Americans' ambivalence toward the United States and Anglo society. The banner headline above a photograph of the U.S. flag that was reproduced on front pages around

Figure 2.2. La Opinón, July 21, 1969

the world reads, *"Dos Yanquis en la Luna"*—Two Yankees—**them, not us**—on the Moon (Figure 2.2).

Although diverse politically—from the progressive stances of the early worker-oriented newspapers to the more conservative politics of the Lozano and López newspapers—early U.S. Spanish language news media portrayed the social dynamism of Mexican and Mexican American communities' adaptation to, and alienation from, Anglo society.

Few U.S. Spanish language newspapers were as long lived as *La Prensa, El Espectador,* and *La Opinión,* and most were not dailies but rather weeklies. Several Spanish language dailies published in Ciudad Juarez, Mexico, and distributed across the bridge in El Paso have been active since 1930s. Another exception is *La Prensa,* a New York daily. In an early example of the bilingual formats discussed in more detail in Chapters 6 and 7, *El Heraldo de Brownsville,* a 6-page daily Spanish language supplement to the *Brownsville Herald,* has been published continuously since 1934; the *Laredo Morning Times,* a south Texas daily, has inserted a 1-page supplement in Spanish continuously since 1926 (Kanellos, 1993, p. 13). Most U.S. Spanish language newspapers (like most English language newspapers), however, did not survive the competition from radio and television that intensified in the 1940s and increased in the decades that followed.

NOTES

1. For overviews of the press of Western European immigrants to the United States, see Kessler (1984), Park (1922), Pozzeita (1991), Miller (1987), and Zubrycki (1992).

2. *El Misisipí,* the first U.S. Spanish language newspaper, was published in 1808 in the major seaport of New Orleans by and for merchants trading in the Spanish colonies of the Caribbean and Latin America (Wilson & Gutiérrez, 1995, pp. 177-179).

3. Park (1922) counts 35 Spanish language newspapers in the United States in 1884 and 60 in 1895, most of them in the southwest.

4. This section draws on a special edition of *America's Review* (1989) about *La Prensa.*

5. González announced his retirement from Congress in 1997.

6. This section draws on García (1989, Chapter 4).

7. For a detailed discussion of the contemporary *La Opinión,* see Chapter 6.

3

History of the Hispanic Audience

The processes that symbolically transformed Latin American residents of the United States and their descendants into a social grouping that is today called the Hispanic audience have their historical roots in the complex, contradictory social history of the southwestern region of the country, a transnational terrain that Guillermo Gómez-Peña has called "a fissure between two worlds . . . but a reality nonetheless, [where] there cohabit two histories, languages, cosmologies, artistic traditions, and political systems which are drastically counter-posed" (Simonson & Walker, 1988, p. 127). This "northernmost point of Latin America" was, in the first decades of the century, the cradle of U.S. Spanish language media and the Hispanic audience.

Audience, in this chapter, does not refer to actual people who listen to the radio, read newspapers and magazines, or watch television and films.[1] Rather, *audience* refers to the social construction that is created and re-created by cultural industry producers, which includes advertisers and marketers. Audience is what is for sale in the media marketplace (Ang, 1991). This historically specific process of categorization and reproduction is imbedded in, and the product of, the large social movements that make up Latin American immigration to the United States and the U.S. response—commercial and cultural—to this immigrant community.

This chapter is centrally concerned with the commercial imperative that motivated the categorization *Hispanic audience.*[2] This political and economic conceptualization of "audiencemaking" is understood more broadly as an institutional and organizational one. "Actual receivers are constituted—or perhaps reconstituted—not merely as audiences but as *institutionally effective audi-*

ences that have social meaning and/or economic value within the system" (Ettema & Whitney, 1994, p. 5, emphasis in original).

A consideration of the historical development of the Latino audience demands a specific contextualization, a problematizing of the production of the Hispanic audience, not only as an economic process but also as a site of cultural contestation.

Another theoretical frame of this chapter is Benedict Anderson's (1986) notion of *imagined communities.* Writing about the spread of nationalism in the late 19th century, Anderson argues that the proliferation of vernacular language print media vitally shaped the emergence of nationalism. Further, Anderson writes, "nationalism and nation-ness" are socially constructed "cultural artifacts,"

> that the creation of these artifacts . . . was the spontaneous distillation of complex "crossing" of discrete historical forces; but that once created they became modular, capable of being transplanted, with varying degrees of self-consciousness, to a great variety of social terrains. (Anderson, 1986, p. 14)

Similarly, this chapter argues that the historically defined creation of the Hispanic audience and, more broadly, the U.S. ethnoracial category *Hispanic,* is the product of the interaction of several social institutions. This chapter focuses on the cultural and economic interactions that created U.S. Spanish language broadcasting and its principal product, the Hispanic audience.[3] Anderson's (1986) argument that the dissemination of mediated messages is key to the creation of cultural categorizations, of "communities," is central to this chapter. The crux of the matter lies in who is doing the imagining. This analysis of the production of the Hispanic audience focuses attention on the interaction of Latinos with the commercial sphere of the dominant society.

In the first part of the 20th century, the creation of the Hispanic audience was concentrated in the southwestern borderlands region of the United States contiguous to Mexico. By late in the century, when the dispersion of the Latino population had become both a demographic reality and a Madison Avenue truism, this regional mapping of the Hispanic audience had been displaced by a national conceptualization of Latinos and their commercial representation: the "Hispanic market." This is not to say that the "mapping" of this audience is today complete. Rather, the historical process of commercially categorizing, of "selling," Hispanics is ongoing. (Its contemporary dimensions are explored in Chapter 4.)

This chapter traces the history of the transnational interaction of U.S. and Mexican broadcasting commercial imperatives and the communities of listeners and viewers that were its consumers, focusing on the representations of Latinos produced by these interactions. Throughout, evolving conceptualizations of the immigrant audience and its place in U.S. broadcasting are contextualized by reference to Latino social history. Intersecting institutional relations, such as those of the broadcasters and the recording and advertising industries, are outlined in an attempt to capture the complex organizational forces that shaped emerging cultural conceptualizations of U.S. Latino societies. The chapter begins with a consideration of U.S. Spanish language radio, where the Hispanic audience developed many of its enduring contours: that of a politically and culturally marginalized yet commercially profitable niche of the U.S. broadcasting industry.

EARLY U.S. SPANISH LANGUAGE RADIO: 1920s, 1930s, 1940s

Until the development of Spanish language radio, Spanish language media in the United States largely had been ignored by the U.S. commercial arena. Spanish language newspapers had been published in the United States since the annexation by the United States of about half of Mexico in 1848. With the exception of the merchant newspapers published in port cities like New Orleans, these early U.S. Spanish language newspapers, often transnational in character, were published by fraternal and other community groups or by U.S. and Mexican political militants that used the broadsheets as weapons in the Mexican Revolution. Although some had advertising support from immigrant enclave businesses, most were sustained by the community groups that sponsored them (Gutiérrez, 1977).

U.S. Spanish language radio differed significantly from the U.S. Spanish language press on the key question of ownership. Unlike newspapers, which were largely owned by members of the immigrant community, radio stations that broadcast Spanish language programming were owned by majority society entrepreneurs. There were no immigrant-oriented radio stations in the 1930s—only immigrant-brokered foreign language radio programs. The principal reason for this was cost. Compared to newspapers, the initial capital outlay for radio stations was prohibitively high. These costs were magnified by efforts by the large-scale enterprises that sponsored early U.S. radio to create barriers to entry to new businesses (McChesney, 1994).

In the first decades of the broadcasting industry, radio station owners found that some hours of the day were not commercially viable. Owners sold these "off hours" for nominal fees to Spanish (and in other parts of the country, other non-English) language radio programmers, who were responsible for acquiring their own sponsors. Owners were hungry for material to fill air time and desperate for the finances to support what was then considered a commercially risky undertaking, an "ether experiment" (Barnouw, 1963). Foreign language broadcasting fulfilled both these needs.

In this early period, radio station owners and advertisers did not think of the Spanish speaking audience as consumers. This can be attributed to the relative isolation of Mexican and Mexican American communities from the dominant society; Spanish speakers were occupationally and residentially segregated from the merchant and business classes, including radio station owners. Until Spanish speakers were conceptualized of as a product that could be sold profitably to advertisers, the importance of Spanish language programming to station owners remained negligible.

The economic and cultural marginality of this programming created an opportunity for the Latino community: With ownership functionally absent and air time restricted to the wee hours, members of the immigrant community were largely left alone to produce radio programs as they saw fit. An immigrant broker/programmer bought air time from the station ownership and paid himself (it is most unlikely this position was held by a woman) with the receipts from the advertising he sold for his programs.

For these immigrant radio producers in the late 1920s and early 1930s, the audience was not in any sense an abstract one. Rather, programming was shaped within the immigrant enclave; face-to-face communication was key. For example, in Los Angeles, broker/programmer Rodolfo Hoyos spent much of his day walking through the commercial district of the barrio, making personal calls on potential sponsors of his one-hour daily live music and talk program. During these sales calls on bakeries and *bodegas,* that day's musical selections or a recent community event that might be mentioned on the air would also be discussed (Gutiérrez & Schement, 1979, p. 5).

During the twenties and early thirties, a period that preceded widely available recordings, radio drama and musical performances were broadcast live by immigrant artists. In this period, a significant portion of Mexican immigration to the United States was "circular." That is, many agrarian workers would spend a season picking vegetables on U.S. farms and ranches and then go back to Mexico, before returning once more to the United States. Southwestern U.S. Spanish language radio programmers, expressing the seamless binationality of their communities, prided themselves on sounding as if they were still in Mexico, featuring performances by Mexican musicians and actors. They did not limit themselves to entertainment programming, however. Responding to the perceived needs of their audiences, these producers often assumed the informational and political advocacy role more commonly associated with immigrant print journalists of the period.

Emblematic of these was Mexican musician and radio producer Pedro González.[4] His radio program, *"Los Madrugadores"* (The Early Risers), began broadcasting from KELW, Burbank, California (just north of Los Angeles), in 1927. The program mixed live performances by Mexican musicians with information about jobs and community services, and it was extremely popular with the city's Mexican immigrant community. González was, by training and predilection, a musician and a performing artist. His response to social and political circumstances of the late 1920s and 1930s transformed him into one of the best-known Mexican American political figures of his generation. In its 1995 obituary, the *New York Times* described González as a "folk hero and social advocate" (p. C20).

Following on the heels of World War I, growing isolationist feelings, and the onset of the Great Depression in the late twenties, the U.S. federal government deported tens of thousands of Mexican immigrants. González's program responded by featuring interviews with the Mexican Consul General and other community leaders who advised the audience—many of them U.S. citizens, or, like González, legal U.S. residents—on their rights. González was arrested in 1934 and subsequently convicted of trumped-up rape charges. He was sentenced to 50 years in prison, all the while protesting his innocence. After sustained protests from the Los Angeles Mexican community, he was released from jail and deported in 1940.

Until González took on the role of defender and advocate for his audience, the owners of the radio station that broadcast "*Los Madrugadores*" had been pleased with the program's ability to fill the 4 a.m. to 6 a.m. slot. González was bringing in new advertising dollars from the immigrant business community. He translated and broadcast advertisements from general market advertisers, such as Folger's coffee, that were discovering the Spanish speaking consumer market. Nonetheless, under political pressure after González's arrest, the radio station discontinued all Spanish language programming. During the early 1930s, U.S. broadcasters in Texas and throughout the southwest also curtailed their foreign language programming in response to harassment directed at ethnic broadcasters, and the imposition of more stringent radio licensing rules (Sánchez, 1993, pp. 183-184).

The reaction of the majority society's political and commercial sectors to the emergent U.S. Spanish speaking audience was contradictory. On the one hand, advertisers had begun to recognize the potential profitability of this audience, and radio station owners discovered that by selling blocks of formerly "dead" airtime to immigrant brokers, they could generate increased revenue. At the same time businesses were courting this community, however, politicians and other majority community leaders were characterizing Mexican immigrants as a threat.

As a cultural complement to mass deportations, in the mid-1930s the Los Angeles district attorney and other government authorities campaigned to ban Spanish from the airwaves. Although many U.S. stations continued to program Spanish language blocks, others wishing to reach Mexican Americans moved their operations to the Mexican side of the border, out of the reach of U.S. authorities (Sánchez, 1993; see also Fowler & Crawford, 1987). The tension created by the contradictory responses of the Anglo establishment to the Mexican community—commercially welcoming, but politically and culturally rejecting—would continue to shape the development of a Hispanic audience.

THE EARLY TRANSNATIONAL HISPANIC AUDIENCE

Without the commercialization of Spanish language music recordings in the United States and Mexico, the commercialization of Spanish language radio would have been significantly retarded; without broadcast outlets in the United States, the profitability of Spanish language recordings might not have been realized. The simultaneity and mutuality of these two developments—which were also occurring at the same time in the nascent general market recording and radio industries—were pivotal in defining the character of U.S. Spanish language radio and its audience. Both can be traced to the commercial acumen of Emilio Azcárraga Viduarreta, a Mexican broadcasting mogul in the William Paley mold, whose defining role in U.S. Spanish language broadcasting is today carried on by his grandson, Emilio Azcárraga Jean.

Emilio Azcárraga began his broadcasting empire with radio stations in Mexico in the 1930s. Through adroit negotiations with the Mexican government and the National Broadcasting Company (NBC), then the preeminent U.S. broadcasting company, he created the first and for decades dominant Mexican radio network (Noriega & Leach, 1979, pp. 17-18). In this same period, he exclusively represented 90% of Mexico's performers (both musicians and actors) in popular radio *novelas,* or soap operas. Azcárraga's early strategic alliances with the Mexican government and with North American entertainment companies helped define the conservative, nationalistic character of the entertainment conglomerate today known as *Televisa* (Hayes, 1993).

In the 1930s, Azcárraga, who *Time* magazine described as combining "John L. Lewis's burliness and the late Wendell L. Willkie's charm," was also a theater owner and the sole Mexican agent for RCA Victor Records (as quoted in Fowler & Crawford, 1987, p. 150). He began transmitting music from his Mexico City station XEW, *La Voz de América Latina* (The Voice of Latin America) to a radio station in Los Angeles, which then relayed it to other U.S. stations. In addition, Azcárraga owned five radio stations along the U.S.-Mexico border that transmitted directly into the United States (Fowler & Crawford, 1987). Mexican artists under contract to Azcárraga would perform in Azcárraga-owned theaters and broadcast stations in Mexico, and subsequently on radio stations in the United States.

Azcárraga's commercial sensibilities—his feel for what would sell to a Mexican mass audience—dominated Mexican theater, musical recordings, and radio. His genius was packaging the nationalistic nostalgia of Mexican popular culture. His export of these commercial formulas to the U.S. borderlands helped shape a U.S. Spanish speaking mass audience. With the success of his U.S. broadcasts, Azcárraga became the largest and most influential producer of U.S. Spanish language radio programming.

Historian Alex Saragoza writes in a forthcoming biography of Azcárraga that the radio programs reflected the media mogul's carefully crafted "conservative nationalism": a pastoral, idealized picture of Mexican life. This view, Saragoza writes, "is perfectly correlated with his [Azcárraga's] commercial interests." Sentimental love songs, for example, became a staple of U.S. Spanish language radio; their teary nostalgia was popular with the Mexican immigrant audience. The songs offer a romanticized vision of Mexico—a country that thousands were fleeing when they came to the United States (personal interview with A. Saragoza, May 1989). For Azcárraga and his fledgling broadcasting empire, the border that separates the U.S. from Mexico was little more than a bureaucratic nuisance. Mexicans who listened to radio lived on both sides of the official separation of the two countries. As social historian Carey McWilliams (1968) writes in *North from Mexico*:

> Essentially these are one people, occupying a single cultural province, for the Spanish speaking minority north of the border (majority in some areas) has always drawn . . . support, sustenance, and reinforcements from south of the border. Our Spanish speaking minority is not, therefore, a detached fragment, but an integral part of a much larger population unit to which it is bound by close geographic and historical ties. (pp. 289-290)

The nationalistic nostalgia of the Azcárraga broadcasts spanned the political demarcation of the border. The audience was, in commercial terms, "captive," because their listening choices were defined by the reach of Azcárraga-controlled stations. The U.S. audience was a bonus for the Azcárraga broadcasting and recording enterprises, which were already returning profits on the Mexican audiences in Mexico. The commercial availability of Spanish language recordings made extended broadcast programming feasible. This, combined with the beginnings of a change in the perception of the audience, prompted the growth of U.S. Spanish language radio in the 1940s.

U.S. broadcasters discovered that the emotional effect of an advertising message delivered in a listener's first learned language and suggestively enfolded in a program of music or drama, evoking the most nostalgic memories of a listener's faraway birthplace, was infinitely greater than the same message in English. Some examples of these 1940s advertisements:

> They speak perfect Spanish at T. Automobile Company. Many Mexicans have bought their cars at T. Company and have been highly satisfied.

> A Mexican will always get a better value from another Mexican. So get your Chevrolet from a Mexican agent at the Central Chevrolet Company. (Landry, 1946, as cited in Gutiérrez & Schement, 1979, p. 6, p. 8)

Whether or not infusing advertising with a sense of linguistic solidarity did in fact increase ethnic sales, what mattered is that the station owners and advertisers believed it to be so. Once radio station owners could profitably sell advertising on Spanish language programs, they dedicated more air time to it. Just 10 years after the inception of Spanish language radio, a 1941 study (cited by Gutiérrez & Schement, 1979, pp. 7-9) found an estimated 264 hours per week of Spanish language radio on 58 radio stations—apparently many of these programs were broadcast weekly, not daily—in four states: New York, Arizona, Texas, and California, mostly in the off hours.

The early Spanish language radio audience in the United States was defined by its "otherness," particularly its continuing close ties to Mexico. When the commercial establishment began to imagine Spanish speakers as members of *their* marketplace, they began to mold Spanish language radio for an imagined audience more commensurate with that of the dominant, majority society. Immigrant program hosts were urged to shorten their commentary and pick up their pace, so as to match better the quick tempo of the new advertisements they were reading. The length of the music selections were shortened also, to make room for more advertising breaks (Gutiérrez & Schement, 1979, p. 21). Raul Cortez, the manager of the first full-time, Latino-owned U.S. Spanish language radio station (KCOR, San Antonio, established in 1947), remembers that "We wanted to sound just like an English station, but in Spanish. In other words we didn't want any of those slow talkers, *mañana* types, with guitars. Spanish, Spanish, Spanish, just like an English station" (Schement & Flores, 1977, p. 58).

Despite their efforts to sound "just like an English station," KCOR's owners found that general market advertisers were not persuaded of the commercial viability of this audience. KCOR asked its listeners to send in boxtops and empty containers to prove to potential advertisers that they spent money and were actors in the marketplace—in short, that they existed. Although some advertisers were willing to buy time on KCOR on the basis of this boxtop evidence, many others were not.

In the postwar period, fledgling audience measurement firms such as Pulse and the Audience Research Bureau (which became Arbitron, today the largest U.S. radio audience measurement firm) did not measure Spanish language audiences. KCOR's manager Cortez prevailed on a college classmate to do a survey, but these statistics did not have the credibility national advertisers demanded. In 1957, KCOR contracted with a New York based national advertising executive and brought him to San Antonio for a crash course on Spanish language broadcasting. Based on his report, KCOR was able to air its first national advertising (Gutiérrez & Schement, 1979, pp. 56-58).

The social chasm between the Spanish speaking audience and the Anglo entrepreneurial class was wide and deep, restricting the contact between the two societies, and so Anglo owners and advertisers had difficulty conceiving of Spanish speakers as actors in their marketplace. The social isolation of Latino communities within the larger society restricted the potential commercial viability of U.S. Spanish language broadcasting.

CHANGING THE IMMIGRANT PARADIGM

Outside the southwest, Spanish language radio shared off-hour time slots with other foreign language radio. In the 1950s, German, Polish, Scandinavian, and other foreign language radio broadcasting began a steady decline. This was largely attributable to the assimilation of European immigrants into the dominant culture. As these peoples were recognized as predominantly English monolingual, the commercial appeal of foreign language radio programs declined; these consumers could be reached with general radio programming and advertising (Warshauer, 1975). As such, foreign language broadcasting was not as attractive to advertisers and thus not as appealing to radio station owners.

During this period, the number of weekly hours of U.S. Spanish language radio doubled. Two thirds originated in the southwest, the region most heavily populated with Spanish speakers. By 1960, Spanish language radio accounted for more than 60% of all U.S. foreign language radio. Spanish was the only foreign language to command entire stations and entire broadcast days (Warshauer, 1975, pp. 84-89). Why was U.S. Spanish language radio growing at a time when other foreign language broadcasting was dying? The answer can be found in the interaction of immigration and language use patterns within the commercial sphere.

Radio station owners and their advertisers were among the first to notice (in commercial terms) that the European paradigm of immigration to the United States was not identical to that of Latin American immigration. Most European immigrants, within a generation or two of their arrival, were socially and economically integrated into the majority culture, losing their European "mother tongue" in favor of English monolingualism. In addition, European immigration to the United States was discontinuous, disrupted by two World Wars and the vastness of the Atlantic Ocean. Once new German immigrants stopped arriving, for example, a generation or so later all but a few reduced their use of German or stopped speaking German completely. Consequently, the market for German language radio dropped off precipitously.

In contrast, immigrants from Latin American countries, primarily Mexico, have arrived in a steady stream (of varying size) to the United States for most of this century (Table 1.1; see also Fuchs, 1990; Grebler, Moore, & Guzman, 1970). Monolingual Spanish speakers settling in the United States renew the life of the language and provide a core audience for Spanish language radio programming. Moreover, because many of the Spanish speaking immigrants have been illiterate and accustomed to participating in oral cultural forms, Spanish language radio has held a special appeal for them (Cortes, 1987).

The subsequent development of television made radio station owners even more receptive to the idea of Spanish language programming. As many advertisers flocked to television, radio scrambled to maintain itself. A principal stratagem is now called "narrowcasting," production and marketing of specially tailored programming targeting demographically distinct audience segments. The Spanish speaking audience is in many ways the ideal specialized audience. Language, race, and their close association with Mexico made the radio audience an easily identifiable audience, though once again it was largely afforded programming in the off-peak hours.[5]

EARLY U.S. SPANISH LANGUAGE TELEVISION

From its inception in 1961 and for the first 25 years of its existence, U.S. Spanish language television was owned, financed, and operated by the Mexican company *Televisa*; U.S. Spanish language television was the U.S. subsidiary of the largest Spanish language media conglomerate in the world.[6] This unusual situation—a developing country annually exporting thousands of hours of television programs to a first world country—provides an early example of the transnational nature of an emerging global media economy. Moreover, it highlights the frame within which U.S. Spanish language television must be examined. The history of U.S. Spanish language television, like that of U.S. Spanish language radio, needs to be understood in the context not only of U.S. media industry economics but of the Mexican media political economy as well.

In the period following World War II, when Emilio Azcárraga might have been expected to be satisfied with his commanding presence in Mexican entertainment industries and his defining role in Spanish language radio programming in the United States, he was instead considering new challenges. In 1946, he formed an association with other Latin American broadcasters to pressure their respective governments to adopt the U.S. model for television licensing and regulation, and not the European noncommercial model.[7] He succeeded, and in so doing planted the seed—in Mexico—for U.S. Spanish language television (Sinclair, 1991).

Azcárraga's radio successes left him well positioned to exploit the new communication technology of television. In 1951, he established his first Mexican TV station and staffed it with singers, actors, and comedians under contract to his radio stations, theaters, and recording labels. In the late 1950s, Azcárraga was beginning to import large quantities of U.S. television programming for dubbing into Spanish for *Televisa* broadcast. The expansion into the U.S. television market was designed in part to reverse the flow of television programming dollars between the United States and Mexico.

From the point of view of a U.S. entrepreneur in the late 1950s, the U.S. Spanish speaking market was so small and so poor a community that it was not considered a market at all. The 1960 U.S. Census counted 3.5 million Spanish surnamed residents. U.S. Spanish language advertising came to only $5 million annually, or less than one tenth of 1% of all U.S. advertising at that time (Valenzuela, 1985, pp. 140-146). From the perspective of a Latin American entrepreneur, in contrast, the millions of Mexican immigrants and Mexican Americans living in the United States were one of the largest and wealthiest Spanish language markets in the world.

For Azcárraga, the U.S. market was an obvious and potentially lucrative arena. *Televisa* was producing profits in Mexico; a U.S. subsidiary would redouble those profits. Moreover, this was not, from Azcárraga's vantage point, a particularly risky business venture. *Televisa*'s various monopolistic companies in Mexico provided him the financial strength and security from which to venture into a promising but unproven market. *Televisa* first approached the three established U.S. television networks, offering them broadcast rights to *telenovelas* (soap operas) and movies, and was rebuffed. Azcárraga's associate René Anselmo (later the president of *Televisa's* U.S. subsidiary, the Spanish International Network) was told by U.S. network executives in the late 1950s that they saw no reason to spend any money on "ghetto time" programming. Anselmo told an interviewer, "In those days, television was always conceived as a mass medium. Nothing was taken into account except a sort of Middletown U.S.A. version of America" (as quoted in de Uriarte, 1980, p. F5).

Finding that *Televisa* programming was not marketable to existing U.S. television stations, Azcárraga in 1961 bought two U.S. television stations of his own: KMEX in Los Angeles and KWEX in San Antonio, creating SIN, the Spanish International Network. Although not holding any broadcast licenses, SIN would become the power center of U.S. Spanish language television by controlling the supply of programming (exclusively produced by *Televisa*) and its financial base, the sale of U.S. national advertising.[8] In the following decade, the fledgling SIN grew to nine U.S. television stations, including four Mexican border stations that broadcast into the United States.[9] The vertical integration of Emilio Azcárraga's transnational entertainment conglomerate gave tremendous economic advantages to early U.S. Spanish language television. *Televisa* had in production, or in its warehouses, hundreds of hours of television programs and movies.

With this financial security as a foundation, SIN took several risks with emerging television technologies: the UHF band, cable television outlets, microwave and satellite interconnections, and repeater television stations. In 1972, a decade before Ted Turner's "superstation" led the growth in U.S. cable television, SIN began expanding the reach of its stations' signal via cable. For example, KWEX, San Antonio, became a regional station with cable distribution throughout south central Texas. In 1972, SIN used microwave technology to interconnect its five western stations, thereby allowing it to sell regional audiences to advertisers. In 1976, SIN became the first U.S. broadcaster to distribute its signal by satellite (Valenzuela, 1985, pp. 153-165).

During its first two decades, SIN was an extension of Mexico's *Televisa*—north of the border. Emilio Azcárraga and, after 1972, Emilio Azcárraga Milmo, the *Televisa* founder's son and heir,[10] exported their Mexican television monopoly to the United States—or perhaps more precisely, expanded their monopoly of Spanish language television north of the Mexican border. The U.S. portion of the *Televisa* empire did not command significant resources. It was, seen from corporate headquarters in Mexico City, simply another facet of *Televisa*'s internationalization project (Molina, 1992, p. 77).

Accordingly, *Televisa*'s audience-making efforts were focused on reaching a regional audience; delivering the *Televisa* signal to all Aztlán, the mythical Mayan territory of ancient Mexico, thus uniting the Spanish language television audience on both sides of the Mexican border. It accomplished this goal through technological expansion that enabled Mexicans and Mexican Americans in the southwestern United States to watch the same *Televisa* programs that Mexicans could in Mexico. SIN executives called their simple and effective distribution system a "bicycle network," a combination of cable and land transport systems. The content was the same commercially proven formula of "conservative nationalism" as that of the elder Azcárraga's recording and radio industries.

In the 1960s and 1970s, virtually every broadcast hour of each SIN station was *Televisa* programming, produced in Mexico: *Televisa telenovelas,* movies, *Televisa* variety shows, *Televisa*'s nightly national news *24 Horas* (24 Hours), and sports programming. U.S.-produced programming was limited; where it existed at all, it was low-cost talk shows (Valenzuela, 1985, pp. 187-192).

Reaching the audience was a simple task, especially when compared with the continuing effort of persuading general market advertisers that the Spanish speaking audience existed and was a good investment. In the 1960s and 1970s, there were large Mexican American (often third and fourth generation) communities with well-established immigrant enclave business districts throughout the southwest (Acuña, 1988, pp. 311-320). Yet, SIN sales representatives often brought television sets with them on sales calls to prove that, first, there was a Spanish language television station, and second, other businesses advertised on it (SIN Launched, 1987).

FROM REGIONAL TO NATIONAL:
HISPANIC MARKETING

SIN, from its inception in 1961 with two television stations in the southwest, had ambitions to produce a national U.S. Spanish language television audience.[11] Crucially, SIN had no competition: The network bought out potential rivals across the country, assuring that no other Spanish language television service was available in the United States. It had a proven program distribution system in the southwest, the region of the country with the largest concentration of Latinos. When new Latin American immigrant flows to the United States began, SIN was well positioned to expand its audience (see Table 1.1, p. 3, this volume).

After World War II and in increasing numbers in the 1960s and 1970s, Puerto Ricans began settling largely in the New York metropolitan area. After Fidel Castro's rise to power in 1961, hundreds of thousands of Cubans fled to the United States, principally establishing themselves in Miami. When SIN in the late 1960s and early 1970s bought UHF stations in New York, New Jersey, and southern Florida, its national expansion was under way.

The SIN expansion was rooted in a primordial understanding of ethnicity: that the Spanish language (and other common cultural attributes such as religion) is an essential tie that binds U.S. Latinos to each other (Espiritu, 1992, p. 4). This conceptualization of ethnicity ignores or submerges structural variables, such as race and class, represented in differing U.S. immigration histories (e.g., Nelson & Tienda, 1985). SIN's interpretation of U.S. Latino panethnicity, which assumed that its Spanish language programming would appeal to all U.S. Latinos, is at the core of its repackaging of a national Hispanic audience for national advertisers.

By 1982, SIN could claim that it was reaching 90% of the Latino households in the United States, with 16 owned and operated UHF stations, 100 repeater stations, and more than 200 cable outlets. Technologically situated and with abundant programming reserves, SIN still needed to sell its concept of a national Hispanic audience to national advertisers.

The notion of a national Hispanic market required a reconfiguration, a remapping of the national commercial map to include the idea of a national Hispanic audience. Advertisers who embraced the Hispanic market broadened their marketing paradigm by acknowledging that Hispanic consumers existed in commercially viable numbers throughout the country, and, crucially, that standard advertising campaigns were not reaching this audience: that specialized advertising on Spanish language media is necessary to reach Hispanics.

The ultimate goal of marketing is to define and name, and so construct, *new* markets. As one marketing textbook states, "Demand is almost never created. It can, generally, only be discovered and exploited" (Stuteville & Roberts, 1975, p. 10). Hispanic consumers had always been there in the marketplace, but they hadn't been "discovered" and conquered as an audience. Crucial to this codification was market research, cross-tabulation of standard demographics and purchasing patterns. By quantifying a group's consumer actions, market research commodifies the group. U.S. Hispanic market research commercially legitimated Hispanic consumers as it produced and delineated Latinos as a profitable audience. Market research made Hispanics intelligible to the mainstream of advertisers, who may not have ever thought about Latinos, much less had any contact with them.

The first national research of the Hispanic market was commissioned by SIN in 1981. The report, *Spanish U.S.A.,* was prepared by the Madison Avenue market research firm of Yankelovich, Skelly, and White. It found that Hispanics are younger than the nation as a whole and therefore well positioned for development of brand loyalty. Further, the market researchers emphasized that although poor, with a median income of about one third less than that of the general population, Hispanics eat out less and spend 25% more of their income on food than the nation as a whole. In short, the marketers found that Hispanics are a young, domestically centered group that is easily and immediately reachable and, because of its relative youth, an even better long-term investment. The report warns potential advertisers to target this population carefully, not with "warmed over English language commercials," but with specifically tailored messages.

Yankelovich et al. (1981) conclude (not surprisingly, given the identity of their client) that the best way to reach the Hispanic market is in Spanish. The Spanish language, they stress, is better able than English to convey the crucial emotional messages of advertising to Hispanics, because it is, as one marketer phrases it, *"la lengua de nuestra alma,"* the language of our soul. In a more practical vein, the marketers also point out that the relatively small number of Spanish language media outlets permits them to claim that they have "pinpointed" this particular consumer market.

This research would not have resonated in the communications industries if the broader popular culture had not also been developing new conceptualizations of Hispanics. Some of the key actors in the reproduction of Hispanics as a national minority were found in government at local, state, and federal levels. The term *Hispanic* began to be used with increasing frequency in the 1970s by governmental agencies to designate Spanish-surnamed or Spanish speaking peoples. In 1980, the Census Bureau used this "generic . . . homogenizing label" for the first time on its survey forms (Oboler, 1995, p. 3).

Yet, despite the efforts of SIN, market researchers, and myriad governmental agencies, the notion of one unitary, national Hispanic market met with early resistance. Anheuser-Busch Inc., manufacturer of Budweiser beer, was the first firm to respond to early Hispanic market research with a 1979 Spanish language print and television campaign targeting the national Hispanic market. This was actually three separate campaigns for the three regional concentrations of national origin Hispanic subgroups. The California, Texas, and the southwest advertisements aimed at Mexicans by featuring cowboys and cactus; the spots targeting Puerto Ricans in the northeast highlighted cityscapes and *salsa* music; Cubans in south Florida were urged to drink Bud with images of palm trees, cigars, and bananas. The varying visual cues were reinforced in each of the three spots with differently accented Spanish speech and national-origin-appropriate music. Other early national Hispanic advertisers, Procter & Gamble, Colgate Palmolive, and Coca-Cola, also used this tripartite formula.

The advertisers displayed their marketing savvy, Hispanic market research executive Isabel Valdes says, by recognizing that "our language is not just Spanish, it is Tex-Mex, Spanglish, Puerto Rican, Cuban" (Personal interview, September 6, 1990). The first national Spanish language advertising campaigns were regionally configured and as such national origin specific: Each component of the advertisement—the visuals, the music, and the narration—was carefully constructed to appeal not to a "Hispanic" consumer, but rather a Puerto Rican, Cuban, or Mexican origin consumer. The imagined community of U.S. Hispanics in this period was distinguished by the Spanish language, overlaid with distinct and specific national foreignness, and overall, by their difference from the dominant American culture.

During the period these advertisements were running, SIN redoubled its efforts to construct its national audience by producing, for the first time, its own U.S.-produced programming. In contrast to the nationality-specific coding of Hispanic national advertising, SIN stressed the "American-ness" of all Hispanics. After 1981 and the start of satellite distribution of its programming, SIN began producing a nightly national news program, the *Noticiero Nacional SIN* (SIN National News) that, despite intraethnic newsroom strains, created a national Hispanic news agenda (see Chapter 5). SIN also sponsored voter registration drives and other public service campaigns that emphasized the U.S. identity of its audience. SIN linked U.S. Hispanics together with common U.S. symbols through its coverage of annual national celebrations such as the Tournament of Roses Parade and the Fourth of July. In addition, network-owned stations began producing local news and public affairs programming.

The new programming strategy represented a limited recognition that the U.S. *Televisa* audience and the Mexican *Televisa* audience had different needs and interests. Moreover, it was an attempt to modify the SIN audience profile from that of a "foreign" or "ethnic" group interested only in programming from Mexico to a more middle-class "American" community participating in the same national rituals as the larger society and consumer market.

National Hispanic advertising strategies began changing in the early 1980s. Clients complained of the costs of doing three separate treatments for one Spanish language national advertising campaign. Advertising agencies responded by devising Hispanic campaigns featuring transnational typography, eliminating nationality distinctive music or Spanish accents, and replacing them with a kind of Latin-beat Muzak and a nationality neutral, "Walter Cronkite"[12] Spanish.

THE "DISCOVERY" OF THE
HISPANIC MARKET (AGAIN)

By the early 1980s, *Hispanic* had been created and re-created as a panethnic national minority group. The categorization of Hispanics as a racially and linguistically unified group, a culturally meaningful "administrative unit" in Benedict Anderson's (1986) phrase, was one of the early signs of the emergence of *Hispanic* as a legitimate topic for national discourse. The general market news media commonplace "Blacks and Hispanics" is another. A national economic recession coincided with increasing Latino population and visibility[13] to produce another in a series of waves of anti-Latino xenophobia, a phenomenon common not only to Latinos, but historically to all immigrant groups to the United States (Handlin, 1979; Higham, 1985). Immigration reform bills were introduced in Congress, as a half dozen states approved English-only ballot measures. This was the social and cultural context for what industry trade magazines trumpeted as the "discovery of the Hispanic market," the institutionalization of Latinos as the Hispanic audience, and the foundation of U.S. Spanish language broadcasting's commercial viability.

At first glance, it is somewhat incongruous that at the same time Latinos were being portrayed in the popular culture (when they were portrayed at all) as poor, marginalized people, they should be "discovered" (rediscovered?) as a market by the Madison Avenue advertising establishment. This view fails to consider the opportunistic logic of consumer market expansion. Hispanics (and in this same period and to a much larger extent, working women and African Americans) became recognized as easily defined and quantifiable, and therefore a commercially attractive group. The commodification of Latinos as the "Hispanic market" is the commercial expression of Latino panethnicity. The packaging of Latinos as an audience to be sold by advertisers is the result of a pivotal shift in perception of Latinos by the commercial establishment.

It is the product of several intersecting developments: a paradigm shift in marketers' reasoning that coincided with the development of narrowcasting and television deregulation.[14] These resulted in the re-creation of Hispanics as a national consumer group and the development of national advertising campaigns designed particularly for Hispanics. Narrowcasting, telecommunications deregulation, and the enormous growth of cable television created a space for the Hispanic market to perform. This in turn made possible advertising campaigns both national in scope and simultaneously narrowly targeted at specific audiences. René Anselmo, the president of SIN, acknowledged that the evolution of national television advertising discourse profoundly changed U.S. Spanish language television. He made the following comments in 1981, 20 years after U.S. Spanish language television's inception:

> In the old days, it was "well, television's a mass medium, and we can't reach everybody so we've got to miss somebody." Now people think of us in terms of ESPN and Ted Turner's thing—now we are seen as that kind of service. (*Television and Radio Age*, 1981)

"That kind of service"—narrowcasting as opposed to broadcasting, and targeted audiences and markets instead of mass audiences and mass markets.

Although the Hispanic market had gained a tiny corner of the U.S. media market, SIN executives still found their first job was to convince potential advertisers that Spanish speakers were attractive market actors (*Television and Radio Age*, 1981). In the context of U.S. Spanish language broadcasting, the continuities are as important as the changes. As Raymond Williams (1983) writes, the descriptor *mass* can denote low quality in addition to high quantity, and the Hispanic market (some 18 million people in 1980), when conceived of as one mass market, remained marginalized by race and culture. In the move toward narrowcasting and specificity, the Hispanic audience continued to be shaped by unresolved tension about how best to conceptualize Latino communities—tension that illustrates the cultural arbitrariness that shaped the categorization *Hispanic*.

Simply put, Latinos, people of Latin American descent, and Latin American immigrants are not born *Hispanic*. Latinos do not generally refer to themselves as *Hispanic*, certainly not among themselves. As a group, they understand themselves as racially and culturally diverse peoples whose primary self-identification is their Latin American nationality, for example, "I'm Mexican," "I'm Peruvian," "I'm Puerto Rican" (Hart-González, 1985; Moore & Pachón, 1985; Nelson & Tienda, 1985; de la Garza, 1992; Rodríguez, 1991; Shorris, 1992; Sommers, 1991). For example, former Congressman Robert García, a New York born Puerto Rican, understands *Hispanic* as an invention of non-Latinos: "When I first came to Washington I saw myself as a Puerto Rican. I quickly realized that the majority society saw me as a member of a larger group called Hispanic" (Moore & Pachón, 1985, p. 2).

Latinismo is strategic and additive. Studies of Latino, Asian American, and Native American panethnicity show that individuals do not cease to identify with their country (or tribe) of origin when adopting a panethnic identity. Rather, individuals assume a panethnic identity in addition to the national or tribal identification (Cornell, 1988; Espiritu, 1992; López & Espiritu, 1990; Moore & Pachón, 1985; Padilla, 1985; Parillo, 1979). In other words, U.S.

panethnicity is born of and develops through interaction with outsiders, that is, with members of the majority society. Although the institutional and commercial transformation of Mexican Americans, Puerto Ricans, and others of Latin American descent has been institutionalized, it remains a contested notion—even among Hispanic marketers.

In 1980, a related source of tension concerning Latino representation remained unresolved on Madison Avenue, in Spanish language newsrooms, and in other cultural production centers (as it is today). It turns on two contrasting approaches to the continuous social process called *ethnicity* or *ethnic identification.* One stresses that Hispanics are a distinct population, quantifiably different from the mainstream. This approach emphasizes the importance of using Spanish language media to reach U.S. Latinos. The second approach portrays Hispanics as simply a group of "Americans" (meaning U.S. citizens) with similar consumer habits and material aspirations as those of the general population. This is a central tension in the national creation and re-creation of Hispanics: between the desirability of ethnic distinctiveness and the definition and targeting it affords, and the reproduction of Hispanics as just another consumer market that happens to speak Spanish.

Perhaps the most telling sign of the depths of these unresolved tensions about the label *Hispanic* is found in the response of U.S. Latinos to this designation. Recent surveys reveal that 15 years after the institutionalization of the term, the overwhelming majority of U.S. Latinos reject it, preferring a national origin self-identification, such as Mexican, Puerto Rican, or Cuban (de la Garza, 1992, pp. 39-40; Rumbaut, 1997).

The first 50 years of U.S. Spanish language broadcasting show how the strategic actions of a monopolistic Mexican firm, *Televisa,* and various U.S. communications companies produced representations of their audience as they carved out commercially viable terrain in the transnational media economy. The symbolic transformation of U.S. Latinos into Hispanics was not brought about solely by the actions of culture industries, but rather in interaction with other social agencies, which also found language, the Spanish language, an apt proxy for race and class and ultimately the core of a consumer categorization. Fundamental economic forces, that is, efficiency and scale, also contributed to these changes in Latino public culture. One streamlined national entity, the Hispanic audience is, simply put, less expensive than three—for advertisers as well as for content producers. (In this context, U.S. Spanish language audience production is representative of broader trends throughout U.S. media. See Barnes & Thomson, 1994; Turow, 1997.)

The historically specific representation of Latinos, first as Mexicans; then as Hispanics but also Mexicans, Puerto Ricans, and Cubans; and finally today as Hispanics of no particular origin, has been a rapidly evolving process of denationalization and then renationalization as members of a social construct called Hispanic U.S.A. Though primarily a product of Madison Avenue and the Census Bureau, this representation is reproduced daily in myriad contexts by the continuing interaction of U.S. Latinos with the larger society. For all the changes in the national mapping of the Hispanic audience, there has also been continuity in its historical production: The Hispanic audience remains on the margins, living in an expanded "northernmost point of Latin America," in the shadows of the United States.

NOTES

1. This chapter draws on Rodriguez (1999).

2. *Hispanic* refers to the label affixed by most U.S. culture industry producers, Hispanic as well as general market media, and governmental agencies, to U.S. residents of Latin American descent. *U.S. Latinos,* or *Latinos,* refers to the people who have been categorized *Hispanic.*

3. I make no claims about the comparability of the social forces of nationalism and ethnicity. Also, I am aware that there is no linear relation between 18th-century newspapers and novels, whose audiences were largely elite, and the popular potentiality of early broadcasting.

4. This information on Pedro González is drawn from a documentary film produced and directed by anthropologist Paul Espinosa (1982), *Break of Dawn: Ballad of an Unsung Hero.* It aired nationally on PBS in 1983.

5. Between 1960 and 1974, the number of radio stations carrying Spanish language programming more than doubled. The great majority (88%) of those stations broadcast in Spanish for only a few hours a week. The remainder carried Spanish language programming for less than half of their weekly broadcast hours (Gutiérrez & Schement, 1979, p. 11).

6. Today, *Televisa* remains the largest single producer of U.S. Spanish language television programming.

7. The commercial model predominates throughout Latin America (with the exception of Cuba), although most governments also sponsor smaller, noncommercial broadcasting networks.

8. The goal was to add SIN's name to the emerging "spot market," the industry name for broadcast advertising purchased station by station (today usually coordinated by an advertising agency), thus permitting concentration on a particular region or demographic group (Schudson, 1984, pp. 66-67).

9. Legally, none of the U.S. broadcast outlets was owned by Emilio Azcárraga, *Televisa,* or any other Mexican national. Foreign ownership of broadcast outlets violates a key provision of the U.S. Communications Act of 1934 (Valenzuela, 1985, pp. 153-168). In 1986, after an investigation by the Federal Communications Commission, SIN was found to be in violation of the Communications Act and was ordered sold. Hallmark

Cards of Kansas City, Missouri, assumed ownership and changed the network's name to *Univisión.* In 1992, Hallmark sold *Univisión* to a consortium that includes *Televisa* as one of the minority owners.

10. In 1997, the founder's grandson, Emilio Azcárraga Jean, inherited the principal ownership of *Televisa.*

11. Unless otherwise noted, the fieldwork for this section was done in September 1990 during a 3-day annual national Hispanic market and trade show. *"Se Habla Español"* is organized by *Hispanic Business,* a national monthly magazine. I interviewed longtime players in the Hispanic market, among them Hispanic marketers for a large Midwest grocery store chain, two national department stores, and a national convenience store chain. In addition, I spoke with the creative directors of two Hispanic advertising agencies and the owner/managers of three Hispanic market research firms.

12. Walter Cronkite, longtime CBS television news anchor and U.S. journalism icon, speaks unaccented, mainstream American (meaning U.S.) English.

13. According to the Census Bureau (Bureau of the Census, 1997), the U.S. Hispanic population was 15 million by 1980 and grew another 53% in the 1980s to 22 million, due in equal measure to increased immigration (Department of Justice, 1995) and a high (relative to the general population) birth rate (Bureau of the Census, 1997).

14. After years of regulatory rulings that had the effect of containing the growth of the U.S. cable television industry (thereby protecting the broadcasting industry), the FCC, beginning in the early 1970s, issued a series of rulings that led to unfettered cable television expansion and thus the growth in narrowcasting formats (Horwitz, 1989).

4

Commercial Ethnicity
The Production and Marketing
of the Hispanic Audience

This chapter specifies the ways and forms in which the Hispanic audience is produced today, analyzing contemporary understandings of the Hispanic audience in Latino-oriented media.[1] The focus of this chapter is the construction of the Spanish language audience by Spanish language media.[2] (Contemporary English language and bilingual Hispanic audiences and media, distinct and separate sectors of the Hispanic market, are the topic of Chapter 7.) The construction of the Hispanic audience shapes as it creates notions of Latino race and ethnicity, U.S. nationalism, and cultural belonging. This chapter ends with a consideration of the economic and cultural structures of *Univisión, Telemundo,* and CBS-*Telenoticias,* Hispanic audience-centered media firms that are the largest producers and distributors of Latino journalism.

In the contemporary U.S. xenophobic culture—exemplified by Californians' passage of Propositions 187 and 209—the Latino representations at the core of the Hispanic audience are inescapably about political and cultural power. Proposition 187, approved decisively by California voters in 1995, sought to eliminate most government services—including emergency medical care—for undocumented immigrants. Proposition 209, approved in 1997, ended affirmative action in California, that is, preferences for underrepresented groups such as ethnoracial minorities and women in government hiring and university admissions. Both these measures were interpreted as racist attacks by most organized Latino political groups and Latino-oriented media.

To discuss the commercial construction of the Hispanic audience is to analyze the political, economic, and social struggles of U.S. society and the Latino
communities that exist within it, as well as the more particularized commercial
media sphere. This chapter examines key practices of some central communication industries, foregrounding issues of power and inequality, mindful that these
popular cultural productions are simultaneously a site of contestation and a cultural resource (Gray, 1995).

The Hispanic audience has been produced through a variety of cultural and
commercial production processes. One of the discrete aspects of these processes
is generally called *marketing,* or, interchangeably in U.S. Latino culture industries, *audience research.* From 1995 to 1997, I interviewed and collected docu-
ments from 17 marketers/audience researchers at various U.S. Latino media
firms: the U.S. Spanish language television networks *Univisión* and *Telemundo,*
as well as several of their affiliates; and Spanish language newspapers and
magazines. The audience researchers made available to me their own market research studies as well as those prepared by such national marketing firms as
DRI/McGraw-Hill; Simmons, Scarborough, Yankelovich et al.; and the A. C.
Nielsen Company. These reports and, more generally, the work of the audience
researchers, are proprietary; the analyses are the exclusive property of the media
firms that produce them or have purchased them. Consequently, although I was
permitted to record our conversations electronically, the marketers will not be
individually identified.

The dominant construction of the Hispanic audience—the discursive concept
that is sold in the marketplace and centrally structures Hispanic media—is racially non-white, linguistically Spanish speaking, and socioeconomically poor.
Despite, and because of, these defining cultural characteristics, Hispanic media
have produced alternative cultural forms within U.S. public culture (Williams,
1980, p. 41). Today, more than 1,000 U.S. television outlets, some 400 U.S.
Spanish language radio stations, 14 U.S. Spanish language daily newspapers,
and dozens of Spanish language monthly magazines and weekly newspapers
have taken their sometimes precarious place within the U.S. media marketplace.

A political analysis of the Hispanic audience is heightened when considering
the identity of the discourses' authors: Most contemporary Hispanic marketers
and audience researchers are U.S. Latinos. Hispanic audience research is constructed by one class of Latinos, college educated and professionally salaried,
symbolically reproducing a saleable product out of the mass of U.S. Latinos,
more than half of whom have not completed high school and whose median family income is slightly more than half (58%) that of white families (Bureau of the
Census, 1996). This is not to minimize the fact that the Hispanic audience is being fashioned primarily for Anglo advertisers and advertising agencies, but
rather to emphasize the class character of Hispanic representation and the lead-

ing role elite Latinos play in its creation. Below, after providing a theoretical context for the consideration of the marketing of ethnicity, I discuss the foundational work of the A. C. Nielsen Company in defining the Hispanic audience, work whose influence is felt throughout Hispanic media marketing.

MARKETING AND ETHNICITY

These are the voices of the men and women, employees of Latino-oriented media firms, who construct and then sell the commercial and cultural commodity commonly called the Hispanic audience:

> We walk a fine line. We want to differentiate [from the general market] but . . . we try to say these are people who want to be Hispanic Americans, but they don't want to lose their Hispanic identity.

> We have come to some retailers and pitched them and said, "We'd like to drive the Hispanic consumer into your store and the way to do that is . . ." And we've heard, "The only Hispanics who come into our stores are the ones who come in here to shoplift."

> We have to quantify our [Hispanic] audience much more than any other market in the country. I don't hear anyone saying to NBC, CBS, ABC, "Prove to me that your viewer is viable." We are always put to the test.

The practice of audience research is constrained and organized by institutional industrial imperatives, but as the above voices show, marketing is immersed in the larger society, as it symbolically re-creates it.

Marketing discourse mobilizes resources for the production of Hispanic ethnicity. Responding to a commercial imperative, ethnic distinctiveness is reproduced in relation to an accepted standard, "The so called 'logic of capital' has operated . . . *through* difference—preserving and transforming difference . . . not by undermining it" (Hall, 1993, p. 353, emphasis in original).

This is the logic of narrowcasting, the production of specialized media for specialized audiences, whether the audience be U.S. Latinos, vegetarians, or sports fans. In the case of the Hispanic audience, a defining tension is produced between the construction of Hispanic as different, and so efficiently targetable, and the construction of Hispanic as just another American consumer group.

Although this study is limited to the construction of the Hispanic audience in the United States, it is important not to lose sight of the transnational Latin American audience, of which U.S. Hispanics make up the northernmost component. This is most clearly seen in television: Roughly half of U.S. Spanish language television programming is produced in Latin America; virtually all the

Spanish language television programming produced in the United States (including the national news, talk, and public affairs programming) is exported to Latin America. Further, Latin American media conglomerates have significant investments in U.S. Hispanic media; for example, *Televisa,* the Mexican entertainment conglomerate, and *Venevisión,* a Venezuelan media firm, each own 25% of *Univisión.* U.S.-owned media corporations (e.g., Time Warner, CNN, CBS, NBC, MTV) produce media that are consumed in Latin America. For instance, in 1997, CBS bought *Telenoticias,* creating CBS-*Telenoticias,* a Miami-based news channel that broadcasts largely to Latin America and produces the national newscast for *Telemundo,* the second largest Spanish language television network in the United States. Considered in this economic and cultural context, the nexus of Hispanic audience construction is not solely difference, which some suggest is a primary characteristic of this period (Harvey, 1989). It is also a profit-maximizing abstraction of similarities—in this case, the common language of the audience.

U.S. HISPANIC PANETHNICITY
AND RACIAL FORMATION

The disappearance of national origin differences in Hispanic marketing and commercial representation (discussed in Chapter 3) erased the distinct immigration histories as well as the differing adaptation and settlement patterns of the three principal Latin American immigrant groups in the United States. Underlying these group distinctions are class differences: The 1960s wave of Cuban immigrants was largely middle class and educated, with many professionals in the group, whereas Puerto Ricans and Mexican immigrants tended to be working class, with many menial laborers among them. The denationalization of Latin American immigrants to the United States facilitated their renationalization as members, albeit marginal, of U.S. society, as a U.S. minority group. This created the cultural space to erase the multiracial Latin American heritage of U.S. Latino communities. Consonant with the class differences mentioned above, first-wave Cuban immigrants were largely of European or "white" ancestry, whereas Puerto Ricans and Mexicans are *mestizo* or of mixed African, native, and white racial heritages.

The submerging of intraethnic national, class, and racial distinctiveness permitted the racialization of the social formation *Hispanic* (Omi & Winant, 1986, p. 61; Winant, 1994). Latino-oriented media did not act in isolation or in a pioneering fashion in the creation of this racial category. The Census Bureau at different times tried and then rejected *Spanish speaking, Spanish surnamed,* and *not black, not white.* In 1980, after rejecting *Latin* as too closely associated with an ancient language, the Census Bureau adopted *Hispanic* (Flores-Hughes, 1996).

Hispanic is a cultural and racial formation that has a provisional, tenuous status in the established U.S. racial bifurcation of black and white. Currently, *Hispanic* is more frequently used in the popular culture than Asian American or Native American, but more often, Hispanic and other references to communities of Latin American descent in the United States are not invoked at all. A prominent exception is the *New York Times,* which follows the Census Bureau when reporting its national polling data, stating, "Hispanic can be of any race."

U.S.-born Hispanic marketers say they personally celebrate intraethnic diversity, professionally endorse denationalized, U.S. Latino panethnicity: "It's less complicated this way. We don't want to be *too* special . . . That's how they think of us anyway. They think we are all the same." Implicitly in the first statement above and directly in the second, these Hispanic audience marketers strategically embrace U.S. Latino panethnicity as central to the intercultural nature of their work; the Hispanic audience is created and re-created relative to the dominant Anglo culture. Central to the Hispanic marketing project is the inclusion of Hispanics in the United States. In that context, language—the Spanish language—is positioned as the primary characteristic of the audience, what makes it commercially valuable. As I further develop below, the Spanish language is also proxy for race and class, non-white race and lower class (Urciuoli, 1996).

QUANTIFYING ETHNICITY:
THE CONTEMPORARY HISPANIC AUDIENCE

U.S. Latino-oriented media companies have found a place in the U.S. media marketplace that—encouraged by deregulation, the growth of cable television, and the development of audience measurement technologies—facilitates niche marketing or media specialization. The definition and marketing of small, internally homogenous audience segments is the product of media industries' desire to increase their "efficiency," that is, their ability to produce and distribute tailored advertising messages to specific, targeted audiences. Smaller, more homogenous audiences, this now-institutionalized argument maintains, offer more value (the ratio of advertising expenditure to specific audience reached) to the advertiser than larger heterogeneous audiences (Barnes & Thomson, 1994; Streeter, 1987).

The dominant characteristic of Hispanic market discourse, like that of markets generally, is numbers, a communication system that privileges that which can be quantified:

Perhaps most crucially, reliance on numbers and quantitative manipulation minimizes the need for intimate knowledge and personal trust. Quantification is well suited for communication that goes beyond the boundaries of locality and community . . . [The] objectivity [of numbers] names a set of strategies for dealing with distance and distrust. (Porter, 1995, p. ix)

Unlike many markets, the Hispanic market is sold across racial, national, social, and cultural barriers, making it apt terrain for the powerfully "neutral" language of statistics. The increased precision (and the perception of the precision) of audience research, including computer-facilitated cross-tabulations, has enabled market research firms to quantify Hispanics and so translate their market value into a language common to all concerned, that is, numbers. The numeric symbol system that fuels the Hispanic (and other) markets is not constructed of objective, uncontested numbers, however. Rather, as is argued below, these symbolic quantifications are strategic and value laden: They reproduce U.S. Latino ethnicity and U.S. nationalism as they create a commercially viable Hispanic audience product.

Hispanic marketers re-create stereotypical characteristics of U.S. Latinos— for example, large families—as attractive consumer traits (Astroff, 1988): "Hispanics consume 143% more milk!" (Simmons Hispanic Market Research, 1996). Aggregate numbers, such as Hispanic population growth figures, interpreted by nativists as threatening ("the tidal wave of immigration") have been reconfigured by market researchers into increases in Hispanic buying power. For example, the amount of goods and services purchased by U.S. Latinos roughly doubled from 1986 to 1996, and stood at $223 billion (Douglas, 1996). These numbers are promoted by the marketers of U.S. Latino media firms and are a staple of the industry trade press.

A primary (but not exclusive) goal of media marketers is to maximize the size of the audience, to create a critical mass of audience numbers. The mass audience for U.S. Hispanic media is made up of people who are thought to reside in a monolingual Spanish speaking world—whether it be in the *barrios* of the United States or Latin America, or in the fluid transnational world of recent Latin American immigrants to the United States. Sociologists and historians have long argued that language is the primary emblem of ethnicity (Edwards, 1975; Fishman, 1972, 1989). In the case of U.S. Hispanic ethnicity, the Spanish language reinforces Hispanic media's "foreign" characteristics. In marketing terms, the Spanish language is the most definable, concrete characteristic of a broadly conceptualized Hispanic mass audience. This mass audience categorization signifies a quality of Hispanic, as well as quantity (Williams, 1983, pp. 192-197).

THE NIELSEN RATINGS AND
HISPANIC AUDIENCE PRODUCTION

The A. C. Nielsen Company (now split into the ACNielsen Company and Nielsen Media Research) is the most influential U.S. audience research firm. It

produces audiences as it measures them. By measuring and so numerically defining an audience, the "ratings" create "audience," an entity that can be sold and
that guides content production. As such, Nielsen numbers, though primarily produced for the television industry, have a determining force throughout U.S.
popular culture production (Ang, 1991; see also Gitlin, 1983; Meehan, 1984).
U.S. Spanish language television, the most lucrative segment of U.S. Latino-
oriented media industries, has long been dissatisfied with its audience quantification services. Since the creation of the first U.S. Spanish language television
station in 1961, executives have complained (in interviews with trade publication journalists) that the A. C. Nielsen Company undercounted the Spanish speaking audience. Additionally, Hispanic marketers said, other commissioned research
had little credibility with general market advertisers and advertising agencies.

   After Hallmark Cards bought the Spanish International Network (SIN) and
renamed it *Univisión* in 1986, re-creating the Hispanic audience so as to increase
its market value became the first order of business. The new president of the network, Bill Grimes, came to *Univisión* after a career at ESPN, which he had
guided from initial conceptualization to its current position as a cable television
standard. Key to his success was persuading the A. C. Nielsen Company to
change its methodology to better measure a television audience newly fractured
by multiple cable channels. The result of his and other cable television executives efforts' was A. C. Nielsen's adoption of the *peoplemeter* technology, which
emphasizes measurement of individual viewing within a household, and so demographic specialization.

   Similarly, the focal point of *Univisión*'s effort to reshape the Hispanic audience was the A. C. Nielsen Company's method of counting Hispanics. U.S.
Spanish language television executives recognized that the Nielsen ratings are
the definitive representation of U.S. television audience, and so the best foil to
Hispanic marketing uncertainty. More than 40 years after the KCOR-AM campaign to prove to San Antonio advertisers that the Spanish language audience
existed (see Chapter 3), national Spanish language television executives were
faced with a similar dilemma. In 1992, *Univisión* and *Telemundo* (the second
largest U.S. Spanish language television network) paid $20 million to the A. C.
Nielsen Company to develop new Hispanic audience measurement techniques.
The U.S. Spanish language television networks did not want to forgo the
monopolistic authority of the Nielsen ratings. Instead, they wanted the A. C.
Nielsen Company to count more Hispanics watching television, especially
Spanish language television.

   Univisión, the wealthier of the two U.S. Spanish language television networks, took the lead in revamping the Nielsen methodology. *Univisión*'s cri-
tique of standard Nielsen audience measurement revealed the inherent fluidity
and cultural biases of objective methodology. A. C. Nielsen relied on Census
Bureau data, which, as the bureau has acknowledged, undercount Hispanics

(Bureau of the Census, 1997, Section 1, p. 1), to identify Hispanic residences. In addition, A. C. Nielsen used largely Anglo, English monolingual enumerators to approach potential Hispanic Nielsen families. Finally, the standard eight-button peoplemeter device was not suitable for many multifamily Hispanic households, where uncles and aunts, as well as grandparents, often occupy the same residential unit. Less concretely, Hispanics, particularly recent immigrants, are not likely to know what the Nielsens are, and may be suspicious of anything that has an "official" aura.

According to Spanish language network executives who were centrally involved in the design of the new ratings system, the new measurement procedures fundamentally altered traditional Nielsen methodology. In the Hispanic Nielsen Pilot Survey performed in Los Angeles (*Univisión*'s largest market) in the spring of 1990, the A. C. Nielsen Company did its own census of Hispanic residences, rather than relying on Census Bureau figures. Bilingual enumerators were sent to homes to explain the importance of the Nielsen ratings, and the number of buttons on the Hispanic peoplemeter was doubled. The new method of counting Hispanics produced a significantly larger Hispanic audience than the standard Nielsen methodology—64% larger. Put another way, the traditional Nielsen count showed that 8% of Los Angeles television sets were tuned to Spanish language programming during the evening time period. The new Nielsens counted 13% of the Los Angeles audience watching Spanish language television. This study has been replicated in 13 markets with similar results. Nationally, the new Nielsen methodology counted 40% more Hispanic television viewers than the previous methodology.

Hispanic television marketers were predictably exultant, celebrating the new Nielsen ratings as a populist affirmation that the Hispanic audience is an audience, like any other:

> What Nielsen allows us to say [to potential advertisers] is, "This is how you gauge every television buy you do. So you can't turn your back."

> The Nielsens are our bible. They validate our position in the market. Nielsen is our number one credible source of data.

> Now we are speaking the same language, the language of eyeballs. "During early prime we can deliver to you this many eyeballs, *efficient* eyeballs."

The goal, these Spanish language television marketers say, is to transform the Hispanic market from a minority or foreign language market to just another market. Or, as one Spanish language television marketer in a major city put it,

> My competition is ABC, NBC, or CBS, or Fox. We are media like anyone else. We are, the Nielsens say we are, 8% of this market. It's not that complicated.

But it is. The new Nielsens have counted more Hispanics watching television and, especially, watching more Spanish language television. The new Nielsen numbers have not, however, translated directly to new advertising billing numbers for U.S. Spanish language television or, for that matter, the targeting of this audience segment by the English language networks. Although billings have increased significantly in the last several years for Latino-oriented media generally and Spanish language television in particular, the Hispanic market remains on the margins of the U.S. media sphere.

According to Latino-oriented media marketers in several large U.S. cities, Spanish language television, print, and radio advertising rates are roughly half those of English language media outlets. Put another way, although the amount of advertising spent on Spanish language and bilingual U.S. media is four times what was spent in 1985 and twice what was spent in 1990, less than 1% of all U.S. advertising dollars in 1997 was spent in the Hispanic market (Cropper, 1998).

The new Nielsen ratings, *Univisión* and *Telemundo* executives hoped, would displace other defining numbers; to a limited extent, they have. Perhaps critically from a marketing perspective, however, according to the Census Bureau, Hispanics are the poorest of the nation's poor. Hispanics have significantly lower median household income, and so less disposable income than any other ethnoracial group in the United States. In 1996, Hispanic family income was $26,179 annually, compared to $26,552 for black families and $44,765 for white families (Bureau of the Census, 1996; Goldberg, 1997). Further, because Hispanic household size is larger on average than that of other ethnoracial groups, individual Hispanic income is even lower, relative to that of the general population (Bureau of the Census, p. 65, table 78).

A widely held perception, which may or may not stem from the above-cited statistics, is that all U.S. Hispanics are poor. One local Spanish language television marketer recalls explaining the new Hispanic Nielsen numbers to a group of potential grocery store advertisers. At the end of the presentation, one asked, "But can they afford to buy cereal?" Sighing, the marketer finished relating this anecdote by saying, "This is still a concept sell. We have to sell the audience."

In promotional materials that *Univisión* marketers use in presentations to potential advertisers, the Hispanic audience is constructed as a U.S. audience, consuming U.S. media, not a foreign or minority audience (much less a transnational one), but an audience who (like you, the potential advertiser) is proud, patriotic, American. This is the central message of a professionally polished *Univisión* video *New America* (1996). It opens with a stylized sequence that seeks to include *Univisión* in a conceptualization of U.S. television networks. A fast-moving, brightly colored bar graph shows the ABC, NBC, CBS, and Fox networks (in descending order), and as the music swells, *Univisión* takes its place as the fifth U.S. television network. This is technically true. *Univisión* does have the fifth largest number of owned and operated television stations in the United States, and it is the fifth most watched television network—by Hispanics.

Below is an excerpt from *The New America* that is saturated with iconic U.S. nationalistic imagery.

> Narrator: Latinos are vital to U.S. economic growth [the Bloomingdales logo, a shot of an American Express Gold Card]. *Salsa* is more popular than ketchup [corresponding visuals]. Yet Latinos still value their culture, the family, their music, their language.

> David Bautista (UCLA School of Medicine sociologist): The question of language is often misunderstood. Latinos want to learn English. And most Latinos do speak some English. When marketing we have to understand where Latinos feel, and most Latinos feel most comfortable in Spanish. If we wish to . . . reach Latinos, we must talk to them in the language in which they feel most comfortable.

After testimonials from Anglo corporate advertisers pleased with the results of their *Univisión* advertising campaigns and an echo of the national anthem, the narrator says, "You can't ignore this market anymore." A slide with "32 MILLION," the Census Bureau's count of U.S. Latinos, closes the video.

This video presentation captures the defining tension of U.S. Hispanic marketing: the desire to portray U.S. Latinos as middle-class Americans; fully participating members of U.S. society (and so its marketing and consumer economies), yet distinctive, definable, and so efficiently targetable. Latinos are inextricably woven into the nation, most speak English, they have lots of kids, and so are vital to the economy. Yet they are special, they speak Spanish, and the best way to reach them is through Spanish language media.

NATIONAL HISPANIC TELEVISION INDEX

As a supplement to the new Nielsen methodology, and in keeping with the goal of selling the audience, *Univisión* commissioned the A. C. Nielsen Company to do a separate study of Hispanic viewers, the National Hispanic Television Index (NHTI). This survey research is used by *Univisión* marketers in combination with other studies (also based on survey research).

Paradoxically, a close reading of these studies reveals a more complicated, and so potentially less marketable, portrait of U.S. Latinos. The NHTI is technically proprietary to *Univisión,* which commissioned it, but is widely available throughout Latino-oriented media industries, as its originators wryly acknowledge.

A major finding of the 1995-96 NHTI (Nielsen Media Research, 1998) is, as the headline in *Univisión* promotional materials proclaims, that "87% of His-

Table 4.1.   Hispanic Households Watching TV

	Total Hispanic Households, Mon-Sun, 6 a.m.-2 a.m.	Total Hispanic Households, Primetime	Total Hispanic Adults, 18-49
Spanish Language	31	35.1	39.4
Univisión	24	27.9	31.8
Telemuondo	7	7.2	7.6
English Language	69	64.9	60.6
Cable	18	15.9	13.6
Fox	17	12.3	11.8
ABC	9	10.6	10.3
Independents	7	5.6	5.5
NBC	6	8.3	8.2
CBS	5	5.9	5.8
Pay Cable	4	4.5	4.2
PBS	3	1.7	1.2

SOURCE: NHTI, September 1994 through May 1995. Shares (percentages) for Spanish language television networks reflect program averages; data for all other viewing sources reflect time period averages.

panics speak Spanish at home," reaffirming the centrality of the Spanish language as the primary marker of Hispanic ethnicity (see Table 4.1).

A careful consideration of the data reveals that more than a third (36%) of this 87% is made up of Hispanics who "mostly" speak English and who are self-designated "bilingual." For example, I, who very occasionally speak Spanish with students and colleagues from my home office (by telephone and electronic mail) and who speak Spanish on the telephone monthly with my grandmother, would be counted as "English mostly" or "bilingual," and thus a Hispanic who speaks Spanish at home. Most sociolinguistic studies would label me "English dominant." Framed in a more advantageous way from the *Univisión* marketing perspective, these data show that 49%, about half of U.S. Hispanics, speak Spanish "only," or "mostly" at home, and so would be most likely to watch Spanish language television.

Other *Univisión*-commissioned data reinforce the notion that the Hispanic market can no longer be defined as linguistically unitary. NHTI data show that just 31% of Hispanic households watch Spanish language television shows (see Table 4.1). These data also show that 69%, or more than two thirds, of Hispanic households watch only English language television.

Another study (DeSipio, 1998) study found comparable results: The majority of U.S.- and foreign-born Latinos watch both English and Spanish language television. Interestingly, both groups value the Spanish language television news the highest of all Spanish language television programming.

Table 4.2.   Spanish Use at Home, Hispanic Adults (18+)

Speak Spanish at home		87%
Spanish only	21%	
Spanish mostly	28%	
Bilingual	16%	
English mostly	22%	
Speak English only at home		13%

SOURCE: Nielsen survey, 1995-96.

The flagship of the *Univisión* network, KMEX-TV, Los Angeles, illustrates the possibilities and the limitations of the new Nielsen method for counting Hispanics.[3] Since the winter of 1995, KMEX (one of the first two U.S. Spanish language television stations, founded in 1961) has won the Nielsen ratings race in three key categories: late afternoon (4-6 p.m.), the main news block (6-7 p.m.), and early primetime (7-9 p.m.). Stated differently, according to ACNielsen media research, more people in the Los Angeles metropolitan area (more "total eyeballs," as the marketers would say) were watching *Cristina,* a *Univisión* talk show, and *Primer Impacto* (First Impact), *Univisión*'s tabloid news program, than were watching *Oprah* or *Hard Copy.* Similarly, the Nielsen ratings show that *Noticias 34* (Spanish language local news) and *Noticiero Univisión* (*Univisión*'s national newscast) had larger audiences than KABC's *Eyewitness News* or ABC's *World News Tonight with Peter Jennings* or the news programs of the other networks, including Fox and PBS. *Univisión telenovelas* (soap operas) like *Dos Mujeres, Un Camino* (Two Women, One Road) had a larger audience than *Seinfeld.* And, crucially, KMEX won the ratings race in the 18-49 demographic group (both male and female), the one most valued by advertisers.

Clearly, this is evidence of the high degree of audience fragmentation in the Los Angeles television market. It is also demonstrable proof of the significance of the new Hispanic Nielsen audience measurement techniques. KMEX's ratings supremacy is also evidence of the limited power of ratings, however. KMEX is number one in the ratings in Los Angeles, but sixth in billings, or advertising revenue. KMEX marketers are not disregarding the Nielsen findings that many Hispanics don't watch Spanish language television. During thrice yearly sweeps weeks (when many advertising rates are set), KMEX runs spots promoting its local news programs on the top-rated Los Angeles English language radio station, a rock station.

The success of KMEX and *Univisión*'s Miami station WLTV-TV, Channel 23, has come at the expense of those cities' English language, general market outlets. At the request of Miami and Los Angeles English language television stations, the A. C. Nielsen Company convened meetings to discuss whether or how the television ratings should be changed. The English language stations' primary complaint was that the Nielsen Hispanic sample did not include enough bilingual Hispanic families (Davies, 1997). As of fall 1998, those discussions continued.

OTHER SPANISH LANGUAGE MEDIA

Following the lead of the A. C. Nielsen Company, Arbitron, the principal U.S. radio audience measurement firm, retooled its methodology for counting Hispanics, with similar results. U.S. Spanish language radio has since the mid-1980s regularly been highly rated, and occasionally top rated, in major metropolitan areas of the southwest and south Florida. The new method of counting U.S. Spanish language radio audiences has increased these stations' audience numbers and altered some conceptualizations of the Hispanic audience. For instance, before Arbitron changed its Hispanic audience methodology, Howard Stern's syndicated radio program led the morning drive time ratings race in Los Angeles, garnering about 5% of the audience. More recently, Pepe Barreto has captured that title with 7% of the 86-station Los Angeles area market. U.S. Spanish language radio, like U.S. Spanish language television, has long relied on language to define the Hispanic audience. Now, again like U.S. Spanish language television, U.S. Spanish language radio audience research is disrupting this decades-old audience paradigm, documenting that many Hispanics listen to English language radio.

In the past, Arbitron sent ratings diaries to random households with Hispanic last names, not considering language use as a variable (Benson, 1996; Jolson-Colburn, 1996; Michaelson, 1996). The new Arbitron research does not assume Hispanic household language use, but rather queries it. The results have gotten the attention of general market, English language radio executives, like this Los Angeles manager:

> We believe that there are three Spanish [sic] markets in this city: those who don't speak English, those who are bilingual, and those who speak only English. All we want is to have all three markets fairly represented in every [ratings] book, by age and by sex. (as quoted in Weinstein, 1996, p. C1)

This manager's comments indicate some tension around a muddy conflation of language, ethnicity, and Hispanic media use, and a nascent desire to bring increasing Hispanic audience numbers into conceptualizations of the general market.

Unlike their broadcast counterparts, which often try to obscure the working-class character of their audience, the three largest U.S. Spanish language daily newspapers, *La Opinión* of Los Angeles, *El Diario-La Prensa* of New York City, and Miami's *El Nuevo Herald,* incorporate these qualities into their niche marketing. Spanish language weekly newspapers such as *La Raza* of Chicago, which has been continuously publishing since 1971, and dozens of smaller, typically short-lived community-based weekly Spanish language newspapers share this philosophy (Moss, 1996). For U.S. Spanish language newspaper audience researchers, the low socioeconomic status of their largely recent immigrant readers is constructed as an advantage. New York's *El Diario-La Prensa* marketers say that the newspaper's clear identification with immigrant readers ultimately caused the failure of *El Daily News,* a short-lived New York daily bilingual newspaper. "They were trying to be everything to everybody and so in the end they were nothing," in the words of one *El Diario-La Prensa* audience researcher.

A marketer for Los Angeles's Spanish language daily *La Opinión* (founded in 1917) asserts that the daily's core audience is "the immigrant flow back and forth . . . Their income level is lower than the general market average, it's lower than the Latino average, it is working class."

Considered out of context, these are extraordinary statements for an audience researcher to make with pride. Clearly acknowledged in these Hispanic marketers' discourse is that this sector of the Hispanic market has relatively low disposable income, which would generally be less attractive to advertisers. In this reproduction of the Hispanic audience, however, U.S. Spanish language newspaper marketers emphasize the special consumer attributes of the Latin American immigrant, for example, relatively more money spent on long distance telephone and electronic money transfer services, airline travel, and immigration-related legal advice.

U.S. Spanish language newspaper audience researchers prominently include politics in their audience definition. Speaking in the context of voter approval of California's Proposition 187 (which would have denied U.S. Latinos many government benefits), a marketer assessed the future of the Hispanic audience in these words:

> The more you isolate and alienate people, the more you are going to draw them into corners, like a Spanish language [news]paper. They [the readers] see you as the only vehicle that they can use to get information.

The principal U.S. Spanish language daily newspapers are financially stable partially because they have reinvented relatively poor recent immigrants as a viable audience commodity. Perhaps just as important is that each draws on the deep pockets of a larger corporation that has perceived the Hispanic audience as vital to its future. *El Diario-La Prensa* is owned by Latin Communications Group, a Hispanic media marketing firm that also owns an advertising agency, three Spanish language television stations, and eight U.S. Spanish language radio stations. *La Opinión* is a product of the Times-Mirror Company, owner of the *Los Angeles Times*; *El Nuevo Herald* is published by the *Miami Herald,* a flagship newspaper of the Knight Ridder chain, which opened another Spanish language (weekly) newspaper in northern California in 1995.

The most numerous local Latino news firms are newspapers and magazines. More than 1,200 of these are members of the National Association of Hispanic Publications (NAHP). Nearly all (93%) are Spanish language newspapers; most are published weekly or monthly. the NAHP lists 14 Spanish language daily newspapers. Overall, the NAHP claims a combined circulation of about 32 million for its member publications—a 150% increase since 1970 (Whistler, 1998). Although several of these publications have existed for generations, and many for 20 or more years, most are new small businesses attempting to capitalize on the growth—and the commercial awareness of the growth—of the Hispanic market.

Closely associated with the recent immigrant conceptualization of the U.S. Spanish language audience is the panhemispheric audience, a discursive construction that is regularly invoked by U.S. Spanish language broadcasters and by the U.S. Spanish language magazine industry. Here again, the Spanish language defines the transnational audience of, for example, the Spanish language editions of such U.S. magazine standards as *Buen Hogar* (Good Housekeeping) and *Cosmopolitan.* Although based in the United States, these Hispanic women's magazines have for decades also been distributed in Latin America. The Spanish language rights to these and other titles (e.g., *Readers Digest, Harpers Bazaar,* and *Popular Mechanics*) are owned by *Televisa*'s *Editorial América. Editorial América* also distributes, in the United States as well as Latin America, *Cristina* (a print version of the *Univisión* talk show) and two youth-oriented glossies, *Somos* (We Are) and *Eres* (You Are).[4]

The newest entrant in the U.S. Spanish language magazine market is *People en Español,* the entertainment glossy. *People En Español* ("How do you say people in Spanish?" sneered one English language Hispanic magazine editor) is published quarterly. It was created in response to the success of the *People* 1995 special edition on the murder of Selena, a Mexican American singer, which sold 400,000 copies. Several weeks later, *People* published (also in English) a special commemorative Selena issue that sold 1 million copies at $3.95 each. As a test for the Spanish language edition, *People* published a special Spanish language edition on Princess Diana (*La Era de Diana*), which sold well. *People En Español* uses the English language *People* format in its coverage of Hispanic celebrities such as Jimmy Smits and Gloria Estefan. Little audience research was done before the inception of *People En Español.* The newsstand sales numbers and owner Times-Warner's deep pockets were apparently sufficient to persuade *People*'s publishers and advertisers of the existence of a U.S. Hispanic audience in both Spanish and English (Nuiry, 1996).

UNIVISIÓN AND *TELEMUNDO:* THE HISPANIC MARKET INSTITUTIONALIZED

At the same time the Hispanic audience was being created and re-created as a commercially viable product, Hispanic-oriented media firms, those culture industries that target the Hispanic audience, were also being reinvented along similar lines. The largest of these firms—in terms of audience size, capitalization, and revenue—are the two principal U.S. Spanish language television networks, *Univisión* and *Telemundo*.[5] This section examines the ownership changes and the role of transnational Latin American and U.S. general market media firms in U.S. Spanish language television.

As noted earlier, U.S. Spanish language TV began as a subsidiary of *Televisa,* a Mexican firm. Twenty-five years later, U.S. law prohibiting foreign ownership was enforced. The sale (to Hallmark) created the first U.S. Spanish language TV network. Even while the network was owned by Hallmark, *Televisa* maintained a key role, though the ownership of Spanish language TV diversified during this period. This section traces the history of these structural changes and the attempted reconfiguration of the Hispanic audience from an immigrant audience to "just another audience." U.S. Latino media institutional development, like the genesis of the Hispanic audience, is a multidimensional process involving Latin American and U.S. media companies and, in the case of *Univisión,* U.S. government regulation.

Federal Communications Commission Orders Sale of SIN

As discussed in Chapter 3, U.S. Spanish language television was founded in 1961 as SIN (Spanish International Network), the U.S. subsidiary of the Mexican entertainment conglomerate *Televisa*—despite the fact that U.S. law explicitly forbids the ownership of U.S. broadcast entities by foreigners. Section 310(a) of the Communications Act of 1934 simply and explicitly bars "any alien or representative of any alien" from holding a station license. Part of *Televisa* owner Emilio Azcárraga's entrepreneurial genius was dedicated to maneuvering around this law. The law prohibiting foreign ownership of U.S. broadcasting firms was not fully enforced until 25 years after SIN's founding.

For Azcárraga and *Televisa,* perhaps the most salient aspect of the law is what it does not address. It does not prohibit the importation or distribution of foreign broadcast signals. In other words, it does not in any way limit foreign ownership of broadcast networks. In effect, the Communications Act does not enjoin foreign ownership of program content; it does, however, prohibit foreign ownership of one mode of transmission of that programming, the broadcast station.

SIN and *Televisa* expeditiously dealt with the foreign ownership prohibition by means of a time-honored business tradition known in Spanish speaking societies as the *presta nombre,* which translates literally to "lending a name," or in colloquial English, "a front." The companies that made up the U.S. subsidiary of *Televisa* were capitalized by *Televisa* money and directed by close Azcárraga associates.[6] Gutiérrez and Schement (1984) speculate about the Federal Communications Commission's (FCC's) apparent lack of interest in the ownership of the first U.S. Spanish language television stations: "An early challenge to the ownership of SIBC was not made, perhaps because of the disinterest of the U.S. networks in the U.S. Spanish speaking audience, coupled with a profitable export market they were enjoying in Mexico" (p. 255).

The vertical integration of Emilio Azcárraga's transnational entertainment conglomerate gave tremendous economic advantages to early U.S. Spanish language television. Additionally, *Televisa* had hundreds of hours of television programs and old movies in its warehouses. Valenzuela (1985) presents evidence that the stations' "debt" to SIN for program acquisition was not paid until 1974, and then not in full. SIN was not clearing a profit, but it was also not paying for its programming. In short, Emilio Azcárraga's deep pockets sustained the early years of Spanish language television in the United States.

Challenges to *Televisa*'s control of SIN began in 1976, when Frank Foucé, Jr., a minority shareholder in SIN, filed suit in U.S. federal court charging that SIN was dominated by foreign interests, namely Emilio Azcárraga and *Televisa* (Wilkinson, 1991). The legal challenges to SIN came at a time when the U.S. federal government had been encouraging minority ownership of broadcast stations. Beginning in the late 1970s, the FCC gave preference to minority-owned companies applying for broadcast licenses.[7] It was in this political context that FCC administrative law judge John H. Conlin ordered the sale of the network SIN and its station group.

The order to sell SIN was met with much excited anticipation by U.S. Latino political groups who felt that for the first time since its inception a quarter century earlier, there was a possibility that U.S. Spanish language television could be controlled by U.S. Latino interests. Frank del Olmo, the only Latino on the editorial board of the *Los Angeles Times,* called on Latino investors to bid for SIN:

> There are many thoughtful Latinos in this country who think the network could do a far better job than it does. Most of the entertainment programming that the net-

work gets from Mexico is no better, and often much worse than the sophomoric pap televised by ABC, NBC, and CBS.

As for community involvement, Christmas telethons to help poor families in the *barrio* are wonderful. But it would be nice too, if local news outlets like KMEX had bigger budgets. Then they could report all year long on the causes of that poverty, like school dropouts, and the consequences, like gang violence. (del Olmo, 1986, p. A22)

Several U.S. Latino investor groups formed, pledging that if their bids were successful, they would keep the network broadcasting in Spanish but with programming more directly responsive to the needs of U.S. Latino communities.

Meanwhile, Hallmark, Inc., of Kansas City, Missouri, the transnational greeting card company, had presented itself to the SIN/SICC representatives on the FCC committee overseeing the sale as a friendly bidder. General managers and other executives were offered employment and stock options if they would lend their support to the Hallmark bid. This ploy, and the solidity of Hallmark's financial plan for the network, apparently swayed the FCC, which awarded the television stations (and later the SIN network) to Hallmark in 1987 on the condition that the stations and the network continue broadcasting in Spanish.[8] Although *Televisa* was forced to give up direct control of U.S. Spanish language television, it remained in a dominant position; despite Hallmark's ownership, *Televisa* still set the parameters of U.S. Spanish language television.

Several Latino groups filed appeals with the FCC seeking to block the sale to Hallmark. The Congressional Hispanic Caucus, the Los Angeles County Board of Supervisors, and the Mexican American Bar Association all cited the public interest and Hallmark's lack of relationship with the Hispanic community in protesting the sale. California congressional Representative Matthew Martinez told the *Los Angeles Times,* "the FCC is violating its own procedures and weakening its policies designed to increase minority ownership of broadcast licenses" (as quoted in Valle, 1987, p. F4).

U.S. minority ownership of media has been a rallying cry of civil rights activists since the 1970s. Media ownership is a powerful symbol of empowerment for U.S. minority communities. Studies suggest that minority-owned stations do not necessarily produce more minority programming, however (Schement & Singleton, 1981). This is not surprising—minority owners operate under the same commercial constraints as any other owners. These constraints include designing programming that will appeal to the largest possible audience that can be successfully marketed to advertisers. The example of U.S. Spanish language television shows that the pluralistic potential of narrowcasting has not been realized in increased racial and ethnic minority ownership, but rather in a partial redefinition of what a marketable audience is.

Instability in U.S. Spanish Language Television

SIN's quarter century of monopolistic control of U.S. Spanish language television ended with the creation, in the late eighties, of the *Telemundo* network. Reliance Capital, which had made an unsuccessful bid for SIN, began the second U.S. Spanish language television network with the purchase of a Los Angeles UHF station, KVEA-TV, Channel 51, and soon after, stations in other major Hispanic population centers, including Miami, Chicago, San Francisco, and San Juan. In the late 1980s, *Telemundo* went public, selling shares on the New York Stock Exchange (Sinclair, 1991, pp. 48-49).

With the Hallmark and Reliance investments, for the first time U.S. Spanish language television was capitalized by U.S., not Mexican, money; also for the first time, there was competition for U.S. Spanish language television viewers. These changes in the market environment of U.S. Spanish language television should not be overstated, however. Both groups were counting on quick and sustained growth of the Hispanic market. These hopes were dashed by the very market forces that originally attracted Hallmark and Reliance to the Hispanic market. Built on shaky financial foundations and market expectations, *Univisión* and *Telemundo* soon faced serious reversals. In 1990, *Telemundo* partner Henry Silverman told an interviewer,

> What I didn't understand because it just didn't occur to me, was that a lot of advertisers would say to me, "I don't want your people in my stores," "I don't want your people in my showrooms," or "I really don't care whether Hispanics buy my products." We went to a major consumer products company and I told this person, "You know, one out of every two children born in Los Angeles is Hispanic," and this person said to me, "Isn't that appalling?" We weren't going to walk out of there with an order. (as quoted in Bechloss, 1990, pp. 30-31; see also Blumenthal, 1990)

In the late 1980s and early 1990s, both *Telemundo* and *Univisión* experienced double-digit annual revenue increases, increases that were partially reflective of increasing ratings (which in turn can be traced to changes in programming). As one trade journalist put it neatly, however, "profitability remain[ed] a matter of statistical conjecture" (Bechloss, 1990, p. 30). Given the above, additional changes in U.S. Spanish language television were inevitable.

In late 1992, *Univisión* announced it had been sold by Hallmark to an ownership consortium headed by Hollywood investor Jerry Perenchio (best known as an early backer of television producer Norman Lear of *All in the Family* fame); Emilio Azcárraga of *Televisa*; and the Cisneros brothers of *Venevisión,* a Venezuelan broadcast company. The sale of *Univisión* brought U.S. Spanish language television full circle; the 6-year Hallmark ownership was ultimately just a pause in the 45-year domination of U.S. Spanish language television by the

Mexican entertainment conglomerate *Televisa*. In sharp contrast with the ownership structures of *Univisión*'s predecessor, SIN, this sale conformed to the letter of the law. *Televisa* and *Venevisión* are minority partners, each owning 25% of the network. Because *Televisa* is the largest producer of Spanish language television programming in the world, however, *Televisa*'s influence in U.S. Spanish language television should not be underestimated.[9] Within weeks of the sale, about 20% of *Univisión* employees were laid off, and three U.S.-produced programs were canceled.

U.S. Latino organizations protested the sale to the FCC. These included the political lobbying groups, the League of United Latin American Citizens (LULAC), and the GI Forum, as well as the Hispanic Chamber of Commerce, the Hispanic Media Coalition, and *Telemundo*. These disparate organizations agreed that the sale "would consolidate one of the world's largest monopolies [*Televisa*]" (Puig, 1992, p. 20), to the detriment of U.S. Latinos. *Univisión* president Joaquín Blaya (who made a losing bid to buy *Univisión* from Hallmark), said at the time, "[the sale] is a recipe for disaster. We [*Univisión*] should be a United States Spanish language television network, not a Latin America network that broadcasts in the United States" (Puig, 1992, p. 22; my translation). The FCC denied the petitioners' request. Within days of the sale, Blaya accepted a job as president of *Univisión*'s competition, *Telemundo*.

Televisa's move to reestablish its power in the United States should be considered in the context of the Mexican entertainment conglomerate's global expansion. The 1992 *Univisión* sale included a provision that would let *Televisa* and *Venevisión* each acquire 50% of *Univisión* if U.S. law were to change to allow greater foreign ownership of U.S. broadcast outlets (Carnevale, 1992). In the early 1990s, *Televisa* bought controlling interests in television networks in Peru and Chile; began selling programming to Spain and Russia (and other countries); created and then closed (at a loss of $150 million—Lopes, 1993) *The National,* a U.S. sports weekly; and purchased *Editorial América,* a Miami-based publishing house that distributes the Spanish language editions of such hemispheric magazine standards as *Cosmopolitan, Good Housekeeping, Harpers Bazaar, Sports Illustrated,* and *Popular Mechanics.*[10]

The critical issue raised by the sale of *Univisión* to a group that includes two of Latin America's largest broadcasting companies is whether the U.S. market can sustain U.S.-produced television diversity. History tells us that without Emilio Azcárraga's deep pockets, or more precisely the deep shelves of *Televisa*-produced programming, U.S. Spanish language television would not exist. Hallmark said in public statements that it sold *Univisión* because it wanted to ensure that its planned expansion into general market cable television would not be curbed by FCC limits on the number of licenses a particular company may hold within a given locale. Another explanation is that Hallmark was losing money on *Univisión*.

Univisión basked in a successful stock offering that followed the Per-enchio-*Televisa* purchase and the increased revenue that resulted from the Hispanic Nielsens. *Telemundo,* the number two U.S. Spanish language television network, spent most of the late 1980s and the 1990s restructuring its debt and re-organizing, after declaring bankruptcy in 1993. Its principal strategy was making programming alliances with other media firms. The initial effort was with *TV Azteca,* the upstart Mexican television network (partly owned by NBC) that was the first serious challenger to *Televisa. Telemundo* bought the U.S. broadcast rights to *TV Azteca*'s bold *telenovelas.* One, *Nada Personal* (Nothing Personal), for example, was a thinly veiled chronicle of the illicit drug trafficking and other government corruption in Mexico's ruling party, the PRI. Although the *TV Azteca* programming gave *Telemundo* a small boost in the ratings in many U.S. markets, overall *Telemundo* languishes far behind *Univisión.* On average in major markets, *Univisión* controls about 85% of the Hispanic Nielsen ratings; *Telemundo* controls about 15%.

In 1997, CBS bought control of *Telenoticias, Telemundo*'s fledgling hemispheric, Miami-based news channel.[11] CBS-Westinghouse was looking for a foothold in the Latin American cable television market. CBS-*Telenoticias,* which looks and sounds very much like *CNN en Español,* its major competitor in Latin America, at this writing was seen in 22 Latin American countries. Miami-based CBS-*Telenoticias* produces a nightly 30-minute U.S. edition, which functions as *Telemundo*'s national newscast (for further discussion of CBS-*Telenoticias* journalism, see Chapter 5). This programming initiative positions the U.S. Hispanic audience as an element—albeit the most important element—of a pan-hemispheric audience.

Also in 1997, a consortium headed by the Sony Corporation and Liberty Media (the programming arm of TCI, a global cable television company) purchased a controlling share of *Telemundo.*[12] *Telemundo,* beginning in the fall of 1998, launched a major reconceptualization of the Hispanic audience, emphasizing production of programming targeting bilingual U.S. Latinos. This development is discussed further in Chapter 7.

JUST ANOTHER AUDIENCE: "BORN-AGAIN HISPANIC" PROGRAMMING

Throughout the *Univisión* and *Telemundo* ownership changes, U.S. Spanish language television network marketers and programmers continued to re-create the Hispanic audience. Although not completely rejecting the profile of the Hispanic viewer as a monolingual Spanish speaker and a relative newcomer to the United States, the television networks took the lead in the production of what *Univisión* (under Hallmark ownership) CEO Joaquín Blaya called "born-again Hispanics."[13] The principal tool in this effort, which continues today, is the production of Spanish language television in the United States. Before 1988, about 6% of *Univisión* programming was produced in the United States, mostly news and public affairs programming; the balance was produced by *Televisa* in Mexico. After the sale of SIN to Hallmark, about half of *Univisión* and *Telemundo* programming is U.S.-produced, a programming ratio that has remained constant. Why the change? The answers lie in the network's desire to produce a different audience for its advertisers.

The production of the contemporary Hispanic audience is a multidimensional process involving many facets of contemporary culture industries: marketers, audience researchers, advertisers—and programmers. Programming, the production of media content for the target audience, is perhaps the most visible facet of the strategic institutional interactions that produce audience. Put another way, the reconfiguring of the A. C. Nielsen Company audience measurement methodology, in and of itself, would not likely have resulted in increased ratings for U.S. Spanish language television.

The core, the mass audience of U.S. Spanish language television, has been historically, and remains today, recent Latin American immigrants and other U.S. Spanish monolingual speakers. These audience members are, because of their generally low incomes relative to the general population, a commercially unattractive group. Hispanics who have been in the United States longer, in contrast, tend to be bilingual, speak both English and Spanish (or only English), have higher incomes, have more disposable income, and are consequently a more attractive audience to sell in the marketplace. *Univisión* CEO (under Hallmark ownership) Joaquín Blaya called these viewers born-again Hispanics (Mydans, 1989). These are bilingual people who have been using more English language than Spanish language media, but for a variety of reasons (affirmative action, racism, family concerns) have recently renewed their feelings of ethno-racial solidarity, and in the process, discovered *Univisión*. Increased domestic programming (and, consequently, less programming imported from Latin America) was the centerpiece of Blaya's strategy of increasing the number of born-again Hispanics in the *Univisión* audience: "We had to develop programming that was relevant to Hispanic Americans living in the United States . . . We developed shows that are American in concept talk shows, newsmagazine shows, the kind you would watch on ABC or Fox" (as quoted in Mydans, 1989, p. F1).

Blaya, a Chilean native, was not exclusively focused on the U.S. audience, however. He simultaneously wanted to produce a panhemispheric audience in Latin America for U.S.-produced Spanish language television programming. "I think there is a tremendous potential for the U.S. Spanish language stations to expand internationally, particularly in Mexico and in Latin America" (as quoted in Puig, 1992, p. 22; my translation). On another occasion, Blaya said, referring to television programming, "If it works here [in the United States], it will work anywhere. I learned that at *Univisión*" (as quoted in Bussey & Arrarte, 1993, p. B4, my translation).

This commercially motivated cultural hybridity seeks to maximize the commonalties (and so minimize the distinctions) of the Latin American and U.S. television audiences. To implement this ambitious programming strategy—attracting middle-class Hispanics while producing programming in the United States for Latin American audiences, as well as maintaining the loyalty of the immigrant audience with which U.S. Spanish language television was built—*Univisión* (and, separately, *Telemundo*) devised a three-pronged programming strategy: imported Latin American programs, U.S. entertainment and talk programs, and U.S.-produced news programming.

The first programming group, which makes up about half the broadcast day for both *Univisión* and *Telemundo,* are the imports. These are the *telenovelas,* serialized soap operas (unlike U.S. soap operas, *telenovelas* have a beginning and an end) that are broadcast for as much as 6 hours a day. In addition, musical variety programs, films, and sporting events (e.g., boxing and soccer) are also largely produced in Latin America.

Producing television programming in the United States (in any language) requires a substantial capital commitment. *Univisión* tripled its domestic programming expenditures in the first 2 years of Hallmark ownership. Investments in U.S.-produced programming were encouraged and rewarded by advertisers, notably Procter & Gamble, which announced that it would buy the great majority of its spots on U.S.-produced shows, not the *telenovelas* (Bechloss, 1990).

Acculturated Latino born-again Hispanics were clearly the predominant imagined audience for the initial group of *Univisión* U.S.-produced programs. Reproductions of proven U.S. television standards premiered in the 1990 television season. *Cita con el Amor* (Date with Love) was modeled on the 1970s hit *The Dating Game. Desde Hollywood* (From Hollywood) was formatted like the general market standard *Entertainment Tonight. Fama y Fortuna* (Fame and Fortune) recalled *Lifestyles of the Rich and Famous.* The late-night *El Show de Paul Rodríguez* (The Paul Rodríguez Show), starring the Mexican American stand-up comic, attempted to re-create the *Johnny Carson Show,* and *Cristina* starred a Cuban American in the role pioneered by Oprah Winfrey. In the late 1990s, the now-proven strategy of producing Spanish language versions of U.S. television standards continued with *Despierta América* (Wake Up, America), similar in format to NBC's *Today* or ABC's *Good Morning America.* This program, which replaced *Televisa telenovelas* (soap operas) tripled *Univisión* ratings in New York and doubled viewership in Miami (Baxter, 1998). These are examples of what Todd Gitlin (1983) calls "recombinant culture":

> Consumers want novelty but take only so many chances; manufacturers, especially oligopolists, want to deploy their repertory of the tried and true in such a way

as to generate novelty without risk. The fusion of these pressures is what produces the recombinant style, which collects the old in new packages and hopes for a magical synthesis. (pp. 77-78)

The formats of these programs have been widely imitated, both in the United States and in Latin America. *Univisión* producers could reasonably assume that their target audience, U.S.-born middle-class Latinos, would be familiar if not with the original programs then with the programs' formula. That lessened the producers' risk; imitating these programs in Spanish made for their novelty.

These *Univisión*-produced television programs were not bald translations of U.S. general market programming, however—interpretations would more aptly describe them. For example, *Desde Hollywood* and *Fama y Fortuna* profiled U.S. Latino and Latin American celebrities as well as U.S. ones (simultaneously translated to Spanish.) *Cristina,* in addition to tearful discussions about family relationships, has devoted programs to sex and sexuality, including a sustained effort to raise awareness of AIDS in Latino communities, topics that have been taboo in many Latino households.[14]

Univisión's Saturday afternoon youth culture block (*Control, Onda Max*), clearly inspired by MTV, features *rock en Español* bands from both the U.S. and Latin America. *Telemundo*'s *Sevec* and *El y Ella* (He and She) employ standard formats, yet are distinctly Latino talk shows. For instance, each has devoted programming to issues concerning contemporary Latino Catholicism. *Telemundo,* under Sony-Liberty ownership, is planning to produce Spanish language versions of *Jeopardy* and *The Dating Game,* as well as a situation comedy, *Sólo en América* (Only in America; Zate, 1998a, 1998b). Also in the late 1990s, *Univisión* is scheduled to introduce a Spanish language Home Shopping Network channel (Pollack, 1997, 1998).

The most successful of these programs (in terms of both revenue generated and U.S. ratings) are *Univisión*'s *Sábado Gigante* (Gigantic Saturday), a variety show, and *Cristina.* Both programs are produced in Miami, and each is seen in 19 Latin American countries. Each, with different production techniques, is careful to appeal simultaneously to U.S. and Latin American audiences. A segment of *Sábado Gigante,* for example, will begin with a shot of host Don Francisco's back as he gazes at a generic crowd, with a voice-over specific to a particular country, before a fast edit to generically panhemispheric studio antics. With a similar tactic, *Cristina* interviews panhemispheric celebrities, such as *Televisa telenovela* stars and Latin American musicians, almost as often as psychologists or designers, fielding questions from the U.S. Latino studio audience.

These programs, the Latin American *telenovelas,* and variety programs, as well as the U.S.-produced and -inspired programs, form the immediate context for the third group of U.S. Spanish language television programming, the news. The same market research that prompted *Univisión* and *Telemundo* executives to target born-again Hispanics stressed that middle-class U.S. Hispanics like to watch the news. In addition to local news programming at the network-owned and major market stations, both *Telemundo* and *Univisión* produce daily "tabloid TV," programs that feature human interest and other dramatic stories. *Occurió Así* and *Primer Impacto* are widely distributed in Latin America and the United States. The national news departments produce two 30-minute daily editions of their national news, one for late afternoon broadcast, one for the evening (10:30 p.m. in the Eastern time zone), as well as a weekly public affairs talk show that airs Sundays.

Most U.S. Spanish language television stations carry 2 to 3 hours of U.S.-produced news programming daily. This is a significant investment in news programming—five times the amount *Televisa* allocated to U.S. news production—and an indication of these networks' determination to re-create the Hispanic audience and Latino-oriented journalism.

NOTES

1. This chapter draws on Rodriguez (1997). It does not examine the production of the Hispanic audience in general market media, first because such representations are sparse, and second because this is a topic deserving its own research (e.g., Turow, 1997).

2. For discussion of the development of U.S. Latino panethnicity see de la Garza (1992), Hart-Gonzalez (1985), Lopez and Espiritu (1990), Melville (1988), Nelson and Tienda (1985), Padilla (1985), Portes and Truelove (1987), Sommers (1991). For a discussion of the role of panethnicity in the production of the *Noticiero Univisión,* see A. Rodriguez (1996) and Chapter 5.

3. WLEW-TV, Channel 23, *Univisión*'s Miami-owned and -operated station, shares in many of KMEX's successes as well as its market constraints. KMEX-TV and WLTV-TV are discussed in Chapter 6.

4. For analysis of the Spanish language women's magazine *Vanidades,* which is distributed in both the United States and Latin America by *Editorial America,* see MacLean (1998).

5. Another U.S. Spanish language television network, *Galavisión,* owned by *Univisión,* is distributed exclusively on cable. It features entertainment, sports, and *Televisa*'s ECO (*Empresas de Comunicaciones Orbitales*) news service. Regional U.S. Spanish language television cable networks include Prime Ticket *en Español,* HBO *en Español,* and MTV *Latino.*

6. The first owners of SIBC, Spanish International Broadcast Companies (later known as SICC, Spanish International Communications Corporation) were three U.S. citizens with long-standing business and personal ties to Emilio Azcárraga: Edward Noble, owner of a major Mexican advertising firm; Frank Fouce (and later, his son, Frank Foucé Jr.), owner of several Spanish language movie houses and theaters in California; and the aforementioned René Anselmo, a longtime *Televisa* employee. Anselmo as-

sumed the presidencies of both SIN and SIBC. Azcárraga retained a 25% interest in SIN (Wilkinson, 1991).

7. In June 1990, the Supreme Court upheld the constitutionality of this policy.

8. Under the terms of the sale, *Televisa,* in addition to cash, was given a guaranteed U.S. customer (the renamed network, *Univisión,* was given a right of first refusal to all *Televisa* programming), free advertising on *Univisión* (for its records and tapes division) for 2 years, and 37.5% of the profits of its former stations (which it never legally owned) for 2 years (Sinclair, 1991, p. 55).

9. Emilio Azcárraga's partner in PanAmSat was René Anselmo, the former president of SIN, who invested the reported $80 million he gained from the SIN sale in the hemispheric satellite.

10. Additionally, after the repurchase of *Univisión* in 1993, *Televisa* announced a partnership with Denver-based Tele-Communications, Inc. (TCI). Together, TCI and *Televisa* could control the emerging Latin America cable television market (Lippman & Darling, 1993).

11. *Telenoticias,* founded in 1994, was a venture of Reuters, *Antena 3 Internacional* (a Spanish media firm), and Artear Argentina Corporation. It was based in Hialeah, Florida (just north of Miami), in *Telemundo*'s network headquarters.

12. Other investors included New York financier Leon Black and Danny Villanueva, a former National Football League player and one of the early managers of Spanish language KMEX-TV, Channel 34, Los Angeles (Pollack, 1997, 1998).

13. After stints as CEO of both *Univisión* and *Telemundo,* Joaquín Blaya left U.S. Spanish language television for U.S. Spanish language radio in 1997. He founded *Radio Unica,* a 24-hour network, which will try to re-create the Hispanic radio audience, traditionally segmented by national origin musical styles, into a panethnic, born-again Hispanic audience with sports, news, and talk programming (Baxter, 1997a, 1997b).

14. An English language version of *Cristina* (a translation of a translation?) had an 11-week run on many CBS-owned and -operated stations in late 1992.

PART II

The Production of
Contemporary Latino News

*The news constructs a symbolic world that has a kind of priority, a certifica-
tion of legitimate importance. And that symbolic world putatively and prac-
tically, in its easy availability, in its cheap, quotidian, throw-away material
form, becomes the property of all of us . . . It makes the news a resource when
people are ready to take political action, whether these people are ordinary
citizens or lobbyists, leaders of social movements or federal judges. This is
the necessity and the promise of the public knowledge we call news and the
political culture of which it is an essential part. (Schudson, 1995, p. 33)*

*One of the things that is most distinctive about television news is the extent
to which it is an ideological medium, providing not just information or entertainment, but "packages for consciousness"—framework for interpret-
ing and cues for reacting to social and political reality. (Hallin, 1986, p. 13)*

*The news tells us not only what happened in the world today but who we are
in relation to that world. (Hallin, 1985, p. 3)*

News has a privileged place within entertainment-oriented media organizations
such as newspapers and television networks. Stated differently, news needs to be
entertaining to generate profit, while also maintaining professional credibility
with the audience (Hallin, 1985, 1986). More broadly, journalism is valued
within U.S. political culture, albeit reviled, but also acknowledged as a player, a
central actor in public conversations about the distribution of power in society.
(As this and countless other studies attest, the study of news is also highly valued
in academic contexts.)

5

Nationhood, Nationalism, and Ethnicity in the Making of U.S. Latino News

The production of Latino-oriented news symbolically denationalizes its intended audience as it renationalizes them as U.S. Hispanics.[1] In this way, the journalists' professional journalistic ethic responds to the commercial imperative of U.S. Latino panethnicity discussed in Chapter 4. At the same time, Latino news explicitly rejects the dominant model of U.S. immigrant assimilation. Latino-oriented journalists—in English, in Spanish, and bilingually—displace the melting pot metaphor of U.S. nationhood, asserting instead that U.S. residents of Latin American descent have needs and interests distinct from those of the general market news audience—and that it is their professional responsibility as journalists to address those particular concerns.

Yet, Latino news is nationalist—U.S. nationalist. Latino news demands and celebrates inclusiveness, the inclusion of Latinos in U.S. society. This journalistic pluralism proclaims the last line of the Pledge of Allegiance, "with liberty and justice for *all*," to counter the symbolic annihilation of Latinos by much of general market journalism. The great majority of U.S. Latino journalists imagine themselves and their audience as communities seeking a just and secure place within U.S. culture, not apart from it, not desirous of any fundamental change in its defining structures.

This journalistic nationalism is centrally constrained, as it is enhanced, by Latino ethnicity. The reproduction of Latino national identity is challenged by symbolic and material ties to other Latin American nations. Although these ties divide Latinos among themselves, the evocation of a collective Latin American heritage also unifies Latinos and provides a link to a founding myth of the United States as "a nation of immigrants."

The concept of nationalism implies commonality, shared values, loyalty to shared ideals; or, as Benedict Anderson (1986) frames it, an "an imagined political community . . . the nation is always conceived of as a deep, horizontal comradeship" (pp. 15-16). U.S. journalistic nationalism, in the case of news produced for Latinos, is at its core paradoxical. The lessening of ties to Latin American nations would seem a necessary first step in the creation or promotion of U.S. nationalism. In this case, however, the maintenance of Latin American heritage is key to preserving Latino ethnoracial identity within U.S. culture.

Nationalism, the construction of a national collectivity, has boundaries that include "us" and exclude "them." "The exclusionary-inclusionary dialectic is necessary to all collective identities' cultural defense" (Schlesinger, 1991, p. 301). This can be seen clearly in public opinion polls taken by Spanish language Latino journalists. Typically listed are three mutually exclusive national ethnoracial respondent categories: *Afro Americanos, Anglo Saxones,* and *Hispanos.* The presumptive audience of Latino journalism does not want to be excluded from the national culture. It does, however, want to maintain boundaries *within* U.S. national culture.

The fluidity and dynamism of this dialectic are evident in Latino-oriented journalism. The tension between U.S. nationalism and Latin American heritage is one of several unresolved and daily reproduced tensions in the production of U.S. Latino news. As Philip Schlesinger (1987) writes, "a national culture is continually developed and the contours of national identity chronically redrawn" (p. 250).

This chapter examines the interplay of U.S. nationalism and Latino ethnicity in the production of news by Latino-oriented journalists. The principal focus is the two nationally distributed Latino television news programs, *Noticiero Univisión* and the U.S. edition of CBS-*Telenoticias,* which together nightly have an audience of about 2 million Hispanic households, by far the largest audience for Latino news.[2]

The discussion below privileges the *Noticiero Univisión,* which commands about 85% of the national Spanish language television audience (Nielsen Media Research, 1998). A specially packaged U.S. edition of CBS-*Telenoticias* serves as the national newscast of *Telemundo* (see Figures 5.1, 5.2, and 5.3). The 30-minute U.S. edition is much like the main CBS-*Telenoticias* feed, but is supplemented by reporting from the United States, including stories about Latin American immigration to the United States and other U.S. domestic news that may not be included in the main feed.

This analysis begins with a consideration of the construction of the journalists' intended audience, the panethnic nation of Latinos. The following section discusses the nexus of Latino journalists' professional ideology, that is, objec-

Figure 5.1. Jorge Ramos

tivity. Subsequent analysis examines the use of the Spanish language in Latino news and the routines, forms, and formats of news productions. The next section examines the principal themes elaborated in the journalistic reproduction of Latino nationalism. The chapter concludes with an examination of the production of Latino national news about Latin America.

LATINO JOURNALISTIC PANETHNICITY

U.S. Latino journalists are deeply embedded in the national journalistic culture and the broader national U.S. culture (Carey, 1986; Schudson, 1995, pp. 1-36). In contrast to many national journalists who have only a "vague image" of their audience (Gans, 1979, p. 230), however, U.S. Latino journalists have detailed conceptualizations of their audience. The journalists' imagined audience is a

Figure 5.2. Maria Elena Salinas

culturally distinct, often oppressed, and exploited people. Latino journalists have also experienced racism and injustice, both personally and professionally. The journalists' conceptualization of and identification with their audience is the central force shaping the production of U.S. Latino news.

Anderson's (1986) "imagined communities" concept is appropriate to the study of this production of culture because journalists cannot know their audience in any direct or immediate way. Thus, the process of "knowing," the construction of the imagined audience, and the mechanisms of that interactive construction are key to understanding the larger cultural and political, in this case, journalistic production. In addition to its defining role in journalistic practice, the presumptive audience is at the center of the economic analysis of Latino news production. Like other media, Latino news must attract and maintain an audience that can be sold to advertisers through the mediation of audience measurement ratings systems. That commercial and journalistic process of audiencemaking (Ettema & Whitney, 1994, pp. 1-19) is centrally motivated by the notion of Latino panethnicity (see Chapter 4).

TELENOTICIAS con Denise Oller y Raúl Péimbert

Figure 5.3. Denise Oller and Raul Peimbert

In 1981, as part of its initial effort to produce a national Spanish language audience in the United States, SIN (Spanish International Network, today known as *Univisión*) launched the *Noticiero Nacional* (National Newscast), the first U.S.-produced Spanish language television news program. (For the previous 20 years, SIN's nightly news had been a rebroadcast of the Mexican network's *Televisa* main news program, *24 Horas.*) The first *Noticiero Nacional* broadcast on June 1, 1981, opened with a dedication from President Ronald Reagan (sitting before the U.S. flag, his words translated to Spanish with subtitles):

> *Buenas tardes.* I want to say how happy I am to help inaugurate the first national news program carried in Spanish . . . I recognize the growing influence of Hispanic citizens in our communities and throughout the nation . . . The Supreme Court once wrote that a free press stands as one of the great interpreters between the government and the people. The medium of television, in particular in a special language newscast, is such an interpreter . . . *Muchas gracias* and *buenas noches.*

The first Spanish language national newscast ended with this idealistic statement, spoken by the anchor:

Our mission is to inform from a Hispanic perspective, emphasizing all that makes us a unique community in this country. This *Noticiero Nacional* SIN will be the means by which all Hispanics communicate with each other . . . throughout the country. (my translation)

Like contemporary Spanish language news, the *Noticiero Nacional* SIN gave over about half its airtime to news of Latin America, and its U.S. news had a "Hispanic angle." *Noticiero Nacional* news director Gustavo Godoy told an interviewer in 1983, "We have the responsibility of allowing Hispanics to become part of the mainstream of the U.S. . . . We cannot allow this group to be misinformed" (Beale, 1983, pp. C85-C86).

The development of Latino panethnicity—which replaces particular, national identities with a Spanish-language-centered U.S. Hispanic one—has been institutionalized in Latino media. The celebration of unity in diversity that is implicit in the commercial construction of Hispanic U.S.A. is relatively simple to reproduce in advertising. News, in contrast, is about politics, and politics is at the heart of intraethnic tensions. Consequently, Latino news emphasizes commonalities among Latinos, re-creating the ethnic group as a community of shared interests. A key challenge for Latino journalists is how to address this notion of their audience as one community while simultaneously respecting differences within the ethnoracial group.

Latino panethnicity is a contested notion in Latino newsrooms, and is minimized, if not dismissed, by many journalists as "marketing talk." Yet it is the touchstone of editorial decisions. Spanish language national newscasts are predicated on the existence of a national panethnic Hispanic market, reconfigured in the context of journalistic practice as a panethnic community of interest. Latino panethnicity is implicit when *Univisión* and *Telemundo* journalists produce stories about the Puerto Rican community in New York City for national broadcast; the presumption is that Mexican Americans in Los Angeles and Cuban Americans in Miami will also be interested in a story about their fellow Hispanics. The presumed panethnic identity of the Latino national audience is a contested one. Nevertheless, Latino panethnicity is a constitutive force in the news production process.

The primary characteristic of *Hispanos* as an imagined audience is that they understand the Spanish language. Moreover, the journalists' presumption is that the audience's interests are *represented* by the Spanish language. This is an understanding of language that expands on the fundamental social function of language as a communicative tool. It is a conceptualization of language as a symbol system that embodies essential characteristics of the ethnic group (Edwards, 1975, p. 17; Fishman, 1989, p. 32). From the journalists' point of view, the audience's demonstrated preference for the Spanish language defines it as a language community, and therefore a community of interest (Anderson, 1986,

p. 29). Former *Univisión* News Director Guillermo Martínez, speaking of the recent Latin American immigrants to the United States that the journalists believe is their core audience, explains in a personal interview,

> They are first interested in *su patria chica* [their hometown], *su nación* [their country], and *su patria grande que es el continente* [their larger country which is the continent, Latin America] . . . Salvadorans are more interested in whether there is corruption in Mexican government or not than they are in the fact that Margaret Thatcher fell in London. (December 6, 1990)

Similarly, one of the constitutive beliefs of the journalists is that their imagined audience is more interested in news of other Latino communities than of African American or European American communities.

The journalists are well aware that national origin and class differences, as well as differences in U.S. immigration histories, can override the unifying power of language in shaping Hispanic self-identification. They recognize that differing political ideologies are at the root of most Latino intraethnic tensions and are not easily disguised. Thus, these Latino national journalists are simultaneously pulled toward two poles. The panethnic pole motivates production for a broad, unified community of interest, for the imagined community that is interested in news of other U.S. Latinos and more interested in Latin American news than in European news. The other, counterpanethnic pole, the journalists explain, pulls them toward production of stories for a more diversified imagined community of interest: Mexicans and border issues; Puerto Ricans and the island's referenda; Cubans and the Castro government.

Recurring controversies concerning intraethnic tensions playing themselves out on the Latino journalistic terrain have made journalists aware of the precariousness of their panethnic project. Many of these stem from the fact that although all national origin Latino groups are represented in the national newsrooms; among U.S.-based journalists, Cuban Americans are overrepresented (relative to their proportion of the Latino population) in management positions in both networks and their respective national news departments.[3] Simmering intraethnic tensions have periodically erupted in national Latino journalism, reminding all concerned of the fragility of the panethnic journalistic project.

In November 1991, a Cuban-born, Madrid-based, syndicated columnist, Carlos Alberto Montañer, as part of his regularly scheduled commentary segment on *Portada, Univisión*'s weekly newsmagazine, offered an analysis of why Puerto Ricans in the United States live in worse economic conditions than other Latino groups in the United States. He said,

> There is probably more than one explanation, but the one that seems most important to me is this: There is a grave family problem in the Puerto Rican ghettos of the

United States, where there are thousands of very young single mothers who try to escape poverty through welfare or through new partners who then leave, leaving behind other children to worsen the problem. (my translation)

The comments provoked immediate outrage from Puerto Rican politicians and community leaders, as well as from non-Puerto Rican Latino leaders. At best, the critics said, Montañer's comments were ignorant and insensitive. Most critics accused him of gross sexism and racism; many demanded his resignation. A coalition of New York City Puerto Rican organizations began an advertising boycott campaign against *Univisión's* New York owned and operated station, WXTV. *El Diario-La Prensa,* New York City's Spanish language daily newspaper, stopped running Montañer's column. Although Montañer apologized for his comments on the following week's program, saying he had been misunderstood, Goya Foods, a Puerto Rican company that caters primarily to the Hispanic market, pulled its advertising from WXTV.

Then-news director Guillermo Martínez complained that Montañer's comments were taken out of context; that, because the controversial commentary was immediately rebutted by another on-air commentator, this was just "good, provocative journalism." Martínez did add, however, that some of Montañer's phrasing was too broad, and thus open to criticism. Several *Univisión* journalists noted with wry grins that the Montañer-Goya incident significantly increased WXTV's ratings.

Another public display of the deeply rooted suspicion and mistrust among varying national origin Latino groups occurred in January 1991. *Univisión's* national newsroom moved from Laguna Niguel, California (south of Los Angeles) to Miami, Florida. The reasoning that led to the move turned on logistical and economic factors involving aerial transportation routes (for taped reports from Latin America), time zones (most U.S. news occurs on Eastern time), and real estate costs (*Univisión* already owned a suitable building in Miami). Guillermo Martínez originally wanted to locate the national news headquarters in Washington, D.C., because, he said, "It is neutral territory," meaning that unlike Los Angeles and Miami, none of the major Latino national origin groups dominates there. That option was ruled out when it was determined that operating the *Noticiero Univisión* out of Washington, D.C., would have been significantly more expensive.

The move was controversial from its inception because, as one Mexican American *Univisión* news staffer put it, "We are leaving behind most of the audience," that is, the Mexicans and Mexican Americans of the southwestern United States, and going to live among "the bad guys," the Cuban exiles of south Florida. *Noticiero* coanchor Jorge Ramos recalled that in the 1980s, a Miami-based

Noticiero SIN was biased in favor of anticommunism generally and the *contras* in particular. He commented,

> We were very concerned about being influenced by the Cuban community and their ideas. Because those are their concerns and other communities have different concerns. We don't want a particular set of ideas to be dominant in the newscast.

The *Noticiero* arrived in Miami in time for the start of the Persian Gulf War. Soon after the war began, Mexican Jorge Ramos became the target of an organized campaign by several Spanish language Miami radio stations long established as among the more strident voices among the Cuban American community. Announcers and callers to radio talk show programs accused Ramos of being "unpatriotic." After several weeks, Ramos confronted his accusers by participating in one of the call-in programs:

> I remember a caller said "I am an architect and a Cuban, but I am first a Cuban and then an architect. And you are a journalist and a Mexican, and before being a journalist you are a Mexican so I don't think you have any credibility."

To decode briefly what the caller was saying: "I am Cuban, anticommunist, and American, and so, politically righteous. You, on the other hand, are Mexican, a commie lover, and have no business talking about my U.S.A."

In one last example of intraethnic Latino tension, Jorge Ramos, like Mexican American *Noticiero* coanchor Maria Elena Salinas (and many of the anchors of local Spanish language television news programs), has fair skin and light hair. Many critics of Spanish language television news see these European (or "Anglo") physical characteristics (which are often associated with Cuban Americans) as a sign of the elite nature of these cultural productions.

These incidents bring into relief decades-old suspicions and resentments among Mexican Americans, Puerto Ricans, and Cuban Americans that turn on political differences of government ideology (e.g., Mexico has traditionally supported Fidel Castro, whom most Cuban Americans vilify), as well as racial, class, and U.S. immigration history differences (see Chapter 3). Latino community leaders and organized Latino political groups publicly participated in these furors through extensive coverage in the Spanish language press, and the English language media located in Latino population centers, such as the *Los Angeles Times,* the *New York Times,* and the *Miami Herald.* Considered more broadly in the context of Latino politics, these incidents illustrate that for Latino community leaders, media are a salient political issue.

The response of nationally distributed Latino-oriented journalists to intraethnic animosity has been to offer their work as a bridge that spans—but does not deny—the material and political differences that characterize the audience, as *Noticiero* coanchor Jorge Ramos elaborates,

> I don't think most Hispanics think of themselves as Hispanics. They think of themselves as Cuban Americans or Cubans, Mexican Americans or Puerto Ricans or whatever. I don't think there is a consciousness that we are Hispanics. I think there is an idea that we share something . . . language . . . the desire to do something in this country better than where we were before . . . I don't think we are a homogenous minority.

Ramos's statement is not a contradiction of Martínez's description of an imagined community of Latino interest, but rather an expression of the contested nature of journalistic panethnicity. In Latino newsrooms, as in the larger society, Latino political and cultural identities are neither unitary nor static, but rather continuously negotiated.

The routines national Latino journalists devise to facilitate daily news production seek to mask and/or avert intraethnic tension. Both *Univisión* and *Telemundo* journalists try to be what they call "national-origin balanced." The stories from the New York bureaus tend to feature news of particular interest to that city's largely Puerto Rican and Dominican population; those from the southwest bureaus tend to feature news of Mexican Americans, and so on. Care is taken not to overload the Miami-based newscasts with Cuban American news. A content analysis of the *Noticiero Univisión* shows that the national origin of Latino soundbites (or news actors) roughly approximates the national population distribution (see Table 1.2), which, according to Nielsen audience research, roughly fits the networks' audience profile. (The journalists were unaware of this "balance" until informed of it by me.)[4]

In a more diffuse way, the journalists, whose offices are in the same building as the networks' sales and promotion staffs, are constantly reminded by posters and videos in the lobbies, by marketing staffers dropping into the newsroom, and by promotional spots that they participate in that the U.S. Spanish language television networks, their employers, are predicated on the notion of a national, panethnic Hispanic market. "*Somos el lazo que une a los Hispanos*" (We are the tie that joins Hispanics) is one *Univisión* musical jingle.

LATINO OBJECTIVITY

Historically, objectivity in U.S. journalism is a product of the progressive era of the late 19th century—a period that saw journalists (as well as lawyers and government officials) re-create themselves as "professionals," holders of expert knowledge and thus a privileged role in society. At the core of this special journalistic knowledge is the ideal of objectivity, the notion that journalism should be value neutral—apart from, disinterested in—partisan politics (Schudson, 1978). Herbert Gans (1979), in his foundational *Deciding What's News: A Study of CBS Evening News, NBC Nightly News, Newsweek and Time,* debunks the myth that grew up around journalistic objectivity, often summarized in the phrase "telling both sides of the story." Gans argues instead that the practice of U.S. journalism is not value-free; that journalists "express, and often subscribe to, the economic, political, and social ideas and values which are dominant in America" (p. xv). Among these values are altruistic democracy, responsible capitalism, small-town pastoralism, individualism, moderatism, and ethnocentrism, by which Gans means, "American news values its own nation above all" (p. 42). Latino-oriented journalists embrace these dominant values, including U.S. ethnocentrism, albeit within a Latino ethnoracial context.

The Latino journalists who produce news specifically for the consumption of a national Latino audience were, if not born in the United States, then educated here, in traditional U.S. journalism schools. As such, they have been socialized to be professionally objective. "The First Amendment [to the U.S. Constitution]," declared one, "is like a religion for me." The practice of objectivity is what makes these Latino journalists *U.S.* journalists. Journalistic objectivity in the context of Latino news is an expression of professional nationalism. Objectivity is the dominant ideology and practice of U.S. journalism, what Hallin (1986) calls "conservative reformism." This is not to say that objectivity is uniformly reproduced in all Latino-oriented news media any more than it is in all general market news media. The ideal of objectivity, particularly the dimension that claims political neutrality, is key to understanding the practice of Latino journalism.

The production of the *Noticiero Univisión* and CBS-*Telenoticias* is a highly routinized, professionally self-protective process (Tuchman, 1972); the result of mutually beneficial elite interactions (Sigal, 1973) that create a nightly capsules of global reality. Objectivity is the nexus of the cultural and ideological commonality that Latino journalism shares with general market journalism. For Latino journalists, like their general market counterparts, objectivity is the emblem of U.S. journalism (Schudson, 1978, pp. 9-10), what makes U.S. journalism special. Journalistic objectivity confers credibility on these ethnic minority journalists; objectivity legitimizes journalists' "expert" positioning relative to the audience and to their general market journalism peers. Closely related to this authoritative dimension of objectivity is its function as a marketing tool (Schiller, 1981).

For Latino journalists, objectivity has special salience. Many national *Univisión* and *Telenoticias* journalists were once employees of *Televisa,* the monopolistic Mexican entertainment conglomerate that is commonly referred to as the Ministry of Culture of the Mexican ruling party, known by its Spanish language abbreviation, the PRI. *Televisa* journalists have rarely been less than fawning in the coverage of the Mexican government, while at the same time largely ignoring government critics. For these journalists, as well as those from other authoritarian Latin American regimes (e.g., Cuba, Argentina), U.S. journalistic objectivity is a professional and political declaration of freedom from government control. A dramatic display of fealty to journalistic objectivity known as the Jacobo affair sparked the creation of *Telemundo,* the second largest U.S. Spanish language television network.

The Jacobo Affair

In 1986, one month after the Federal Communications Commission (FCC) ordered *Televisa* to sell its U.S. stations (SIN), *Televisa* reassigned Jacobo Zablukovsky, the anchor of *Televisa*'s premier news program *24 Horas,* to a new U.S.-based news service. ECO (*Empresas de Comunicaciones Orbitales,* Orbital Communications Companies) would absorb the U.S. staff of the *Noticiero Nacional,* SIN's nightly newscast, and would be broadcast to the United States and throughout Latin America. Jacobo Zablukovsky is the icon of Mexican television news, and as such the embodiment of *Televisa*'s progovernment, censoring journalistic philosophy.[5] *Televisa* readily accepts official guidelines on how specific news items are handled, and rarely criticizes the government directly (Riding, 1984).

Word of Zablukovsky's pending move to the United States came just months after Zablukovsky had presided over *Televisa*'s silence about charges of voter fraud in the border state of Chihuahua, as well as silence about large-scale protests over the Mexican government's handling of the destruction caused by the 1985 Mexico City earthquake. Both stories were covered extensively by general market U.S. news media. SIN sent crews to Chihuahua when it realized *Televisa,* its own network, was not following the story. Within days of the news that Zablukovsky was coming to the United States, more than half the staff of SIN's *Noticiero Nacional* resigned,[6] including news director Gustavo Godoy,[7] who said at the time, "The perception in many quarters in Mexico and this country is that *24 Horas* is a vehicle of the Mexican government. It is not seen as an objective newscast" (Riding, 1984).

Former SIN journalist José Diaz Balart[8] also framed his resignation in terms of journalistic philosophy:

> From the first day we have refused to compromise our journalistic integrity and we are quitting because of ethics, because of freedom of the press, because of dignity, and because we cannot guarantee the objectivity of SIN news. (as quoted in Meluza, 1986, p. B1)

Spanish language radio stations in Miami and Los Angeles received hundreds of telephone calls supporting the resigning journalists and critical of Zablukovsky and *Televisa* journalism generally (Valle, 1986). Zablukovsky never took up his post in the United States.[9] *Univisión* Washington bureau chief Debbie Durham, while rejecting *Televisa* journalism ethics, cautions against over-interpreting the Jacobo affair, noting that the SIN journalists who did not resign (including herself and Jorge Ramos) did not want to abandon their personal and professional investments in the first U.S. Spanish language television national newscast by "throwing out the baby with the bath water."

When *Televisa* reestablished its position in *Univisión* in 1992, the journalists were again worried about editorial interference, especially in reporting from Mexico. Judging from *Televisa*'s history, these are reasonable concerns. As of this writing, the pressure to curb criticism of the Mexican government and the PRI has not been evident in the newscast. *Univisión*'s long-standing association with *Televisa* did interfere with the U.S. network's coverage of the Zapatista revolt, however. Correspondent Bruno López had difficulty convincing Zapatista leaders that he was not a spy for the Mexican government because he worked for an organization, *Univisión,* formerly owned by *Televisa* (López, 1997).

Objectivity and Advocacy

According to many (both national and locally distributed) Latino journalists, objectivity and its opposite, advocacy, are topics of daily discussion in Latino newsrooms. The question is often framed as, "Do we give the audience what they want or what they need?" Gustavo Pompa Mayo, one the founders of *Telenoticias,* declared in an interview that all Latino-oriented journalists, that is, those who make news specifically for Latinos, are "by definition" advocates for the Latino communities. Debbie Durham, *Univisión*'s Washington bureau chief, when asked about advocacy in the *Noticiero Univisión,* responded,

> Where we do come into some of that [advocacy] is when we select the pieces we are going to do based on who the imagined audience is . . . We are dealing with a unique audience; a large part of our audience has been ignored in other media . . . There is an education part to what we do.

Alina Falcón, executive producer of the *Noticiero Univisión,* addressed the question of Latino objectivity and advocacy this way:

> This is going to sound corny: we almost have a special responsibility to our community. Perhaps more so than the English [language] stations. They [our audience] rely on us not only for information but for assistance in every day living . . . We do

focus more obviously on the viewpoint of the Spanish [language] community issues because that's who we are. I don't think individual journalists should be advocates . . . Perhaps the news organization, or the newscast in general, because it is
geared and focuses on the Hispanic audience, will focus more on Hispanic issues.
And if that means we become advocates for the Hispanic community, then so be it.

Falcón concluded this train of thought with these words:

If they [U.S. English language network news] choose only to cover the Hispanic
community when negative issues come up, which is pretty much true, are they being objective?

Falcón's question is frequently asked by Latino-oriented journalists when
queried about their professional objectivity. To paraphrase and summarize their
answers: "General market journalists who ignore or distort Latino communities
are not truly objective. We (Latino-oriented journalists) justifiably and self-
consciously privilege the particular needs of Latino communities, needs that are
largely ignored by general market journalism." This is not, however, a rejection
of traditional journalistic objectivity. Rather, Latino journalism absorbs the objectivity ideal into a public service orientation. This vision of the U.S. nation,
and Latinos' place in it, simultaneously spotlights the reality of Latino marginalization and the journalists' aspirations for Latino communities.

Form and Content

The distinction between journalistic form (presentation norms) and content is,
to a large extent, an arbitrary one. As Michael Schudson (1982) writes,

The power of the media lies not only (and not even primarily) in its power to declare things to be true, but in its power to provide the forms in which the declara-
tions appear. News in a newspaper or on television has a relationship to the real
world not only in content but in form; in the way the world is incorporated into un-
questioned and unnoticed conventions of narration, and then transfigured, no
longer a subject for discussion but a premise for any conversation at all. (p. 98)

Further, and as a complement to the citation above, Daniel Hallin (1985)
writes of political content symbolized in forms of journalistic narratives,

Political structure thus comes to be embodied in certain ways of speaking about
politics, conventions of communication that in their turn profoundly affect the
possibilities for political discourse in the society. (p. 831)

This analysis of the form and content of U.S. Spanish language television news draws on the two theoretical perspectives cited above.

The particular Spanish language employed by the national journalists is part and parcel of the cultural and political assertions these newscasts are making about Latinos. Similarly, the journalists' choice to adopt U.S. broadcast journalism conventions is an expression of their affiliation with traditional U.S. journalistic norms. The analysis below, which occasionally separates some elements of form and content in the interests of clarity, presents the Spanish language as well as various narrative conventions (e.g., soundbites) and workaday news production routines as interactive, constitutive elements of the news production process.[10]

Language

The Spanish language is the broadest symbol system employed by *Univisión* and CBS-*Telenoticias* in the production of their newscasts. The *Noticiero Univisión* and the U.S. edition of CBS-*Telenoticias* legitimatize the Spanish language as a language of U.S. political discourse and thus Spanish speakers as legitimated U.S. political actors. At the same time, the Spanish language in these newscasts is a declaration of Latino ethnic identity. As *Noticiero* executive producer Patsy Lorris Soto said in a personal interview, "We are committed not only to maintaining the Spanish language, but to improving it, and teaching it" (June 4, 1991, my translation). For instance, both the *Telenoticias* and *Univisión* news stylebooks contain a brief English-Spanish dictionary that translates legal terms for the U.S.-educated journalists. For example, a (judicial or court) ruling is, in Spanish, *un fallo.*

Other illustrations of this "teaching" of the Spanish language in news production include the journalists' avoidance of *Spanglish,* or the mixing of English and Spanish in a sentence. Quite common, however, is the sequential use of English and Spanish in common phrases. For example, during a story about a new immigration regulation, it was explained that a $1,000 "cash, *efectivo*" fee was required at time of application. Other examples: "Planned Parenthood o *planificación familiar,*" and "*fútbol,* soccer." A more politically charged example of intermingling Spanish and English is the use of the English abbreviation for the U.S. Drug Enforcement Agency, DEA (a highly visible presence in Latin America), as a Spanish language word, pronounced *deh-ah.*

The English language is rarely heard on these U.S. newscasts—at least not at full volume. A standard television convention (known as "up and under") permits English to be heard for 1 or 2 seconds (at most) before the journalists' translation of the soundbite to Spanish "covers" it. At large public events (e.g., political demonstrations), field producers carry placards that read *"¿Habla Español?"* (Do you speak Spanish?) as a way of identifying Spanish speakers for "person in the street" interviews. When traveling abroad, producers carry similar signs, such as *"Spanski?"* in Russian, resulting in the surprising sight of Russian persons on the street speaking perfect Spanish on U.S. television news. Of course, no production strategy is necessary when interviewing members of the Hispanic Congressional Caucus, Latino members of the presidential cabinet and White House staff, or those Anglo federal (or other government) officials who speak fluent Spanish (like U.S. Senator Christopher Dodd or former Reagan administration official Elliot Abrams).

In the audiencemaking context of U.S. broadcast journalism, the Spanish language often has a counterpanethnic function; particular Spanish language accents and diction, although mutually intelligible, identify the speaker's particular national origin. The journalists are committed to using a Spanish language that will appeal to and be understood by all Hispanics, as *Noticiero Univisión* coanchor Maria Elena Salinas explains,

> We are careful selecting our words, looking for a universal Spanish language, if there is such a thing. [The audience] are all correct in their own countries, but a Colombian might say something that I know a Mexican would not understand. So we try to use a word that is both grammatically correct and understood by most people. Or we use two words, this or that. Or we use both.

For instance, *mosquito o zancudo* was the topic of one *Univisión* newsroom discussion. *Mosquito* is the word used by Mexicans and Mexican Americans to mean a buzzing, biting insect. *Zancudo* is the word used in some other Latin American countries. Because Mexicans and Mexican Americans make up the great majority of the *Noticiero* audience, *mosquito* was used on the newscast. Majority audience does not always rule. When the question was *foco o bombillo* (lightbulb), or *chile o ají* (peppers), both words were used in the newscast.

Panethnic Spanish is a question not only of vocabulary but also of accent and intonation. *Telenoticias* and *Univisión* journalists speak "accentless" Spanish, a product of their interaction with Latinos of various national origin groups and their professional training. For those who immigrated to the United States as adults, losing their national accents and replacing them with a nationality-neutral accent was a conscious effort. Mexican-born *Noticiero* coanchor Jorge Ramos reports that his Spanish accent is achieving its panethnic goal:

> People think I am from their country . . . What is so interesting is that people look at me as their own. [After all these years in the United States] I have developed some kind of an accent that people can translate to their own culture.

Like the nationality-neutral Spanish accent, the journalists' use of the collective personal pronoun, *nosotros* (we) and *udstedes* (you or your) is a symbolic bridge between audience members, as well as between the audience and the journalists. The use of collective personal pronouns in U.S. media is hardly unusual; *U.S.A. Today* and various network promotional campaigns come to mind.[11] Exceptions are made to this rule in U.S. general market broadcast news during war time or national celebrations, such as the Olympics. The use of *we* on these occasions marks the events as special. In sharp contrast, the use of personal collective pronouns in the *Noticiero Univisión* is routine; it is part of the journalistic lexicon.

In the context of the *Noticiero Univisión,* that of a multinational, panethnic, ethnoracial minority cultural production, the symbolic salience of these pronouns is worth particular note. *Nosotros* and *udstedes* reference a particular unitary group, U.S. Hispanics. Examples include *Nosotros en este pais* (We in this country) and *Tenemos que prepararnos* (We need to prepare ourselves). Every evening, among the first words of the *Noticiero* is *su* (your). An announcer says, *"Este es su Noticiero Univisión con Jorge Ramos y Maria Elena Salinas"* (This is your *Univisión* newscast). The word *su* (your) in the initial seconds of the *Univisión* newscast is an invitation and a declaration of ownership—to the audience. *Univisión*'s use of collective, personal pronouns signals that the journalists and the audience together are the insiders, the legitimate actors, in this newscast.

Formats

Luis Calle, former executive producer of the *Noticiero Univisión* and currently executive producer of CBS-*Telenoticias,* stated very simply in a matter-of-fact tone that the "American network" (ABC, NBC, CBS, CNN) newscasts are the "best in the world." The presentation norms of the *Noticiero Univisión* and CBS-*Telenoticias* are emblematic of this fully acknowledged mimicry. Or, as Armando Guzmán, Washington, D.C., correspondent for the *Noticiero* and one of the original correspondents of SIN's 1981 *Noticiero Nacional,* recalls, "In the beginning, when we chose the same [sound]bites as CBS, we knew we were on the right track."

These Spanish language journalists do not question the audiovisual presentation conventions of U.S. television news; they instead credit these production routines for bringing dramatic unity to the plot and narrative of news stories (Carey, 1986, p. 148). Rapid, predictable, narrative pacing—both within stories and within the nightly news program—are, in the journalists' eyes, what makes for compelling television. The daily production meeting (where that evening's program is outlined) is one of the very few times the journalists will, without any embarrassment, speak Spanglish: *"el* kicker," (a light feature, traditionally the last one in the newscast), *"los* supras," (the captions that identify soundbites), and the most damning word in this lexicon: "boring!" The *Noticiero Univisión* and CBS-*Telenoticias* are, without the soundtrack, indistinguishable from a general market news program: from the traditional attractiveness of the anchors, to the shots of Washington correspondents signing off in front of iconic buildings, to the "quick cut" pace of the editing, and the framing of head shots, the *Noticiero Univisión* and CBS-*Telenoticias* look like U.S. news programs, which, after all, they are.

A comparative content analysis of the *Noticiero Univisión* with ABC's *World News Tonight with Peter Jennings* (A. Rodriguez, 1993, 1996) shows how the narrative structure of the reports on the two networks is identical. This speaks to the formulaic nature of U.S. national television news and *Univisión*'s embrace of it. The 100-second dramas (or "wraps") are identically structured and, in many of the Washington, D.C., stories, feature the same cast of characters. Forty-one percent of the soundbites on the *Noticiero Univisión* are of government officials; 41% of the soundbites on ABC are of government officials.[12] Additionally, the two newscasts employ a similar proportion of "unknowns" (Gans, 1979), or otherwise anonymous people, to "humanize" news coverage; 28% of *Univisión* soundbites are of unknowns, whereas 27% of ABC's are. These similarities highlight the journalistic and commercial imperatives that shape both programs. Both ABC's *World News Tonight with Peter Jennings* and *Univisión*'s *Noticiero Univisión* (as well as CBS-*Telenoticias*) attempt each evening to maximize their audience by producing—within the boundaries prescribed by journalistic objectivity—a largely inoffensive, professionally consensual news program.

Equally significant content similarities between the two programs illustrate the fundamental professional commonalities of the *Noticiero Univisión* and ABC's nightly national news program. For both newscasts, the largest single U.S. subcategory is stories produced in the networks' Washington, D.C., bureaus. For both networks, these are their largest bureaus, reflections of the nation's capital-centered political culture, headquarters of the legislative, judicial, and executive branches of the federal government. The privileging of government officials as news actors within the *Noticiero Univisión* is one indication of the political orientation of the program; despite cultural differences, *Univisión* is a participant in the "nationalization of newsroom culture," where national news organizations are in continual interaction (Schudson, 1991, p. 271). This interplay reaffirms and reinforces the tacit social consensus among national journalists about what news is and how it should be represented.

Univisión institutional news sources for U.S. and international news (with the exception of Latino and Latin American news) are the same as the general market networks and those of the larger national news culture. *Univisión* and *Telenoticias* journalists begin their working days listening to news radio, watching CNN, and reading the *New York Times* and the *Wall Street Journal*. (Bureau producers and correspondents read their local newspapers also, both English and

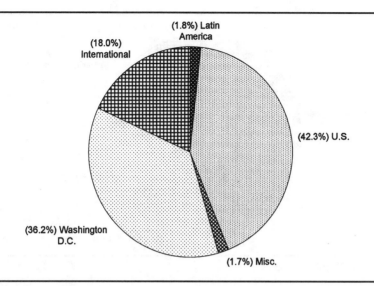

Figure 5.4. ABC Topics

Spanish language.) They also regularly read *Time, Newsweek,* and *U.S. News and World Report.* In the *Univisión* and *Telenoticias* national newsrooms in Miami, the Associated Press and Reuters print newswires are available on the computer monitors atop each desk, as are video newswire rundowns from CNN and ABC. Signs that these national newsrooms are somewhat different than others are the Spanish language *Noti-Mex* newswire from Mexico, the *Imevisión* video newswire (also from Mexico), *CNN en Español* feeds, and the (U.S. and Latin American) Spanish language newspapers on the assignment editors' desk. The national (video and print) news services' interpretation of U.S. and international news is wholly accepted by the journalists. These are among what Tuchman (1978) calls U.S. journalists' "web of facticity," that is, what the journalists believe to be factually "true." The national Spanish language television journalists might quibble with issues of style and emphasis, but they do not question the fundamental framing or analysis presented by the news services.

Story Selection

Despite the similarities outlined above—similarities in format, emphasis on government officials as newsmakers, and similar institutional news sources—there are significant foundational differences between the Spanish language national news programs and their general market counterparts. Figures 5.4 and 5.5 illustrate the sharply contrasting contours of the story selection process of the

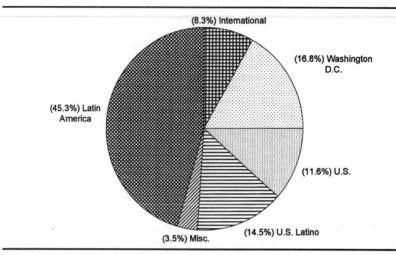

(8.3%) International

(16.8%) Washington
D.C.

(45.3%) Latin
America

(11.6%) U.S.

(3.5%) Misc.

(14.5%) U.S. Latino

Figure 5.5. Univisión Topics

Noticiero Univisión and ABC's *World News Tonight with Peter Jennings,* show-ing with broad strokes their most obvious differences.[13]

Focusing first on the category "U.S.," note that this is the largest categoriza-tion of ABC stories. When this category is combined with "Washington, D.C.," the content analysis shows that despite its name, *World News Tonight with Peter Jennings* is nearly four fifths (79%) about the United States.

The same calculations for the *Noticiero Univisión* show that less than half (43%) of this U.S. national newscast is about the United States. The *Univisión* newscast contains slightly more news about Latin America than about the United States. Turning to the Latino category, ABC devoted just over 1% of its air time to coverage of Latino communities and issues (immigration, affirmative action, and the like), whereas the *Noticiero* gave this category about 15%. (This understates the proportion of time the *Noticiero* devotes to Latino news, because Latinos are often featured in stories coded "U.S." in this content analysis.)

These story selection differences between *Univisión* and ABC turn on the dif-ferences between the social and economic status of the presumptive audiences of the Spanish language networks and the general market networks. Specific ex-amples illustrate this difference. Although both ABC and *Univisión* produced comparably framed (strategic, inside-the-beltway stories) about Zoe Baird, President Clinton's unsuccessful nominee for attorney general, *Univisión* pro-duced extensive interviews with Baird's undocumented employees and used the controversy as a "peg" for a series on Latino domestic labor. Similarly, when George Bush chose Jack Kemp to be his running mate in 1992, Latino journalists, like general market journalists, mentioned Kemp's relative youth and his experience as a cabinet housing secretary. Latino journalists also gave prominent play (in the first or second sentence) to the fact that Kemp had come out publicly against California's anti-immigrant Proposition 187. In another example, the *Noticiero* and CBS-*Telenoticias* each night offer summaries of the day's Wall Street activity, and report on the day's dollar exchange rate for nine Latin American nations.

These examples and others discussed below are representations of ethnicity as a point of view, a worldview, a distinct cultural and political lens through which news is produced. *Univisión* and CBS-*Telenoticias* coverage of Latin America and Latino communities is also an expression of Latino ethnicity that highlight the social ambivalence of this ethnic minority group, marginalized participants in two worlds. Moreover, the construction of these stories—topics not generally included in general market national newscasts—illustrates how Latino national journalism is a special case within U.S. journalism. The unifying theme of these stories is their symbolic inclusion of Latino communities, and issues of presumed interest to them, in U.S. society.

LATINO NEWS

Unlike U.S. news, there is no professional journalistic consensus about what national Latino news is; there is no wire service "day book" listing the day's most important national Latino news events. To the extent that this question has been addressed by general market national journalists, the consensus is, apparently, that news about Latinos is not national news.[14] Latino national journalists reject this exclusion and adapt—but do not fundamentally alter—general market routines and conventions for Latino-oriented news. The journalists' recognition of the social marginalization of their audience informs the alternative vantage point from which Latino news is made. This section examines the intersection of traditional U.S. journalistic values and a decidedly untraditional news topic: Latinos.

As shown in Figure 5.5, the *Noticiero Univisión* dedicates approximately one seventh of its air time to news of Latino communities, slightly more time than it gives to news that emanates from the nation's capital, the traditional center of U.S. news production. These stories tend to be more nuanced and thoughtful, less cut and dried than other U.S. reporting.[15] The social status of the Latinos that populate these stories is markedly different than that of the general U.S. news population: Newsmakers tend not to be Latino. An analysis of the content of the *Noticiero*'s U.S. Latino stories groups them into two broad categories. In the first, Latinos illustrate traditionally conceived U.S. news stories, such as those about the national economy, public school education, or new discoveries in the health sciences. The second group of stories, principally concerning Latin American immigration to the U.S. and Latino civil rights, are rarely included on the mainstream national news agenda.

The first, most frequently produced, type of *Univisión* and *Telenoticias* Latino stories uses Latinos and Latino communities to illustrate an otherwise traditionally conceived story. For example, instead of interviewing European Americans in suburban Chicago about a federal study on the increasing incidence of measles, as ABC did, the *Noticiero Univisión* sent a correspondent to a Latino neighborhood in San Francisco. This inclusive gesture draws U.S. residents of Latin American descent into the public sphere of U.S. civil society, in this case as a group that will be affected by government policies that have been developed in response to a potential measles epidemic. This particularizing of the news for the Latino audience does not alter the mainstream conceptualizations of newsworthiness that shape these stories.

Former *Univisión* news director Guillermo Martínez declares, "We only cover Hispanics when they make news." In this instance, the Latinos who were making news were Latino physicians, Latino public health officials, and Latino parents of young children. Other examples of this mode of Latino national television news include reports on the Latino national unemployment rate (which is regularly about twice the general population figure) produced the day national general population unemployment figures are released. These reports include the comments of Latino demographers and labor economists.

The *Noticiero*'s coverage of Latinos in the electoral arena of U.S. politics as voters, candidates, and elected officials is a special case of the inclusive mode of *Univisión* U.S. Latino news. *Univisión* journalists are supporters of U.S. electoral processes. In this they are no different than their general market colleagues. The *Noticiero*'s unblushing advocacy of the inclusion of Latinos in U.S. electoral politics sets it apart from its mainstream counterparts, however. Some examples: Coverage of Latino candidates is unabashedly favorable; a recurring theme of this political coverage bemoans traditionally low Latino voter registration rates; the *Noticiero* demonized California Governor Pete Wilson for his advocacy of Proposition 187, which would have denied many government services to undocumented immigrants, in much the same manner as the English language networks (as well as *Univisión*) demonized Saddam Hussein.

Univisión's U.S. Latino electoral political coverage somewhat submerges the panethnic ideal. It explicitly recognizes the divergent political orientations of the three major national origin groups; to do otherwise would bring into doubt the journalists' credibility. Like ABC, *Univisión* employed a national election pollster in 1992 and 1996. The polls' respondent categories were *votantes de descendencia anglosajona,* voters of Anglo-Saxon ancestry and *negros,* blacks. *Hispanos,* Hispanics, was subdivided into three groups: *Cubano-americanos,* Cuban Americans; *Mexico-americanos,* Mexican Americans; and *Puerto-*

riqueños, Puerto Ricans. Consistently throughout the presidential election season, poll results showed significant differences among the three groups, with Clinton leading by wide margins among Puerto Ricans and Mexican Americans, and Bush ahead by somewhat smaller percentages among Cuban Americans.

Whereas *Univisión* Hispanic vote coverage highlights the desirability of Latino participation in U.S. political processes and institutions, *Univisión* coverage of immigration issues focuses on the exploitation of Latinos by those same institutions and practices. In these stories, the journalists position themselves, in the 19th-century progressive tradition, as populist muckrakers. These stories, although often critical of aspects of U.S. society, are not oppositional. They do not seek to change the structures or ideals that govern U.S. society. Rather, *Univisión* journalists' conservatively reformist aim is to expose rule breaking for the benefit of their audience.

Both Spanish language television networks devoted considerable and sustained coverage to the elimination of affirmative action in higher education in Texas and California. When the "Hopwood" federal district court decision striking down affirmative action in Texas, Louisiana, and Mississippi was announced, it was the lead story—the story journalists consider to be the most important story of the day. When Jesse Jackson led an Austin, Texas, rally and march protesting the ruling, it was the first story on that night's *Noticiero Univisión*. Although it was clear from these stories' placement in the newscasts, and in the context of the continuing coverage of the issue, where the sympathies of the journalists lay, each story contained soundbites and narration presenting the point of view of affirmative action's opponents.

A defining presumption of the construction of the national Latino panethnic news audience is that a heritage of immigration—second only to the Spanish language—is the basis of a profound sense of commonality among U.S. Latinos. Further, the imagined audience's interest in immigration is broadly conceived; they are interested in Haitian immigration to the United States and Latin American immigration to Spain, as well as the primary focus, Latin American immigration to the United States. One 1992 *Noticiero* opened with these words:

> We begin this newscast today with the story of the tragedy of all of those who flee their country. Today this touches us particularly closely because we are talking about people from Cuba and people from Mexico. People who are fleeing because of political or economic reasons and whose goal is almost always the same: the United States. We have two reports. (my translation)

One report was about the increasing number of Cuban nationals arriving in south Florida on homemade rafts. The second concerned the enslavement of a group of Mexican immigrant men in Texas. In both reports, the immigrants, whose health was seriously compromised by the circumstances of their immigration, were framed with respect, if not admiration. "We are telling truths that are not usually told," remarked one *Noticiero* journalist, referring to a report about unauthorized Mexican immigrant garment workers in Texas who organized a strike, and at great risk to themselves and their families forced the repair of their workplace.

A series of special reports that aired in October 1992 (during sweeps week) was titled "Scapegoats." It was introduced with these decidedly unobjective words:

> We are going discuss how immigrants are used as the scapegoats for the economic ills of the United States, and the intensification of racism against Hispanics as the economic situation worsens. (my translation)

The series, anchored from Los Angeles, included reports on the "militarization of the border with Mexico." In each of these reports, the views of the relevant government agency, xenophobic community leader, or anti-immigrant political candidate were represented. In these stories, which were produced in accordance with traditional journalistic guidelines, the issues divided into two sides, with both represented. *Univisión* and CBS-*Telenoticias* journalists posited themselves as defenders of Latin American immigrants in the United States, many of whom do not have a public voice.

The defense of the imagined audience is often fused with the journalists' service orientation; they feel it is their professional responsibility to assist their imagined audience. This is clearly seen in the national Latino journalists reporting on the legislation approved in 1996, officially named the Illegal Immigration Reform and Responsibility Act and the Personal Responsibility and Work Opportunity Act. After detailed coverage of the bills' passages through Congress, Latino national television journalists gave extensive coverage (often daily) to the bills' consequences in Latino communities throughout the country. These bills, as originally approved, took away disability payments and food stamp eligibility from legal immigrants who were not U.S. citizens. In addition to covering the organized protests against these measures in Latino communities (and Washington, D.C.), the two Spanish language national newscasts visited nursing homes and senior citizen centers in Latino neighborhoods, producing stories about the *efecto devastador* (the devastating effect) the new law would cause among many Latino elderly. The stories were often framed as unjust and tragic tales of upstanding people, who after decades of paying taxes in the United States were being denied a peaceful old age by anti-immigrant Anglo politicians. Of course, proponents of these measures were also represented in these stories.

"*La Nuevas Reglas del Juego,*" the new rules of the game, was the title of a week-long 1997 *Noticiero Univisión* special series on the new immigration law. Changes in U.S. immigration law are a regular and ongoing feature of all

Latino-oriented news. Many of the reports, with a keen perception of prevailing political discourse, frame the new immigration law as "anti-family [values]." Profiles of families being separated (e.g., a deported mother returning to Mexico as the father, a U.S. citizen, remained with the U.S. citizen children in the United States) were interspersed with detailed coverage of congressional efforts to soften the law. Coverage of immigration law often included interviews with immigration attorneys about particular aspects of the law, including the toll-free phone numbers of national organizations to contact for assistance. This professional journalistic service orientation is a principal focus of local Latino news.[16]

A final example illustrates how although presumed interest in immigration is key to Latino journalistic audiencemaking, it cannot mask profound intraethnic differences. Cuban American Republican Congressional Representatives Lincoln Diaz Balart and Ileana Ros-Lehtinen proposed giving amnesty (and so legal residency) to recent Nicaraguan immigrants as part of the Refugees From Communism Relief Act (also included were some eastern European and former Soviet Union immigrants). Other members of the Hispanic Caucus, led by Puerto Rican Democratic Luis Gutiérrez, were outraged, saying that if any Central Americans were to be given amnesty, then all should be, including immigrants from El Salvador and Guatemala.[17]

A final note on the production of nationally distributed Latino-oriented news about the United States: Although *Univisión* journalists' personal and professional experience prevents them from wholly embracing the "contemporary ideology of American racial openness,"[18] their ethnocentrism and professional ideology constrain their challenge of it. The soundbite analysis shows a larger proportion of people of color overall on *Univisión* than on ABC—35% of *Univisión* soundbites are of Latinos, as compared with less than 1% of ABC soundbites.[19] Yet, news actors who are African or Asian American are 50% less represented on *Univisión* than they are on ABC.[20] In other words, the *Noticiero Univisión,* although modifying the white ethnocentrism of general market newscasts, is primarily shaped by its own ethnocentrism and does not fully confront the racial myopia of the dominant society.

LATIN AMERICA NEWS

Like Latino news, news of Latin America is not a regular feature of the U.S. national television news. As with their coverage of Latino communities, *Univisión* journalists embrace traditional U.S. journalistic ideology in their Latin American reporting—with modifications. Nearly half, 45%, of each *Noticiero Univisión* is about Latin America, whereas just under 2% of ABC's *World News Tonight with Peter Jennings* is taken up with news of Latin America. This enormous disparity in story selection is the clearest direct evidence of the distinct worldviews of these two U.S. television networks. Further, 48% of the

Noticiero Univisión lead stories, the stories journalists consider to be the most important story of the day, are Latin America stories. The significance of these reports is their inclusion and prominence in a U.S. newscast; they declare simply and unambiguously that in *our* world Latin America matters. The Latino-oriented journalistic construction of that world is one in which Latino life in the United States is interwoven symbolically and materially with Latin America.

One startlingly clear example of this Latino-oriented worldview happened when Pope John Paul II visited Cuba in early 1998. All the general market U.S. television networks sent correspondents and crews, as well as anchors, to Cuba to cover the story (as did *Univisión* and CBS-*Telenoticias*), a sign of the event's journalistic importance. The U.S. general market networks sent their anchors back to the States when the Monica Lewinsky story broke, however. The U.S. Spanish language network anchors and special technical crews stayed in Cuba to produce extensive coverage of the Pope's Cuba visit (including live broadcasts of the Havana papal Mass). *Univisión* and the U.S. edition of CBS-*Telenoticias* also produced extensive coverage of the Lewinsky story.

The production of Latin American news is key to Latino journalists' professional self-concept as objective journalists. As mentioned above, many Latino television journalists are former employees of SIN and *Televisa,* and are daily reinforcing their rejection of what they believe is severely compromised journalistic practice. These journalists relish the opportunity to work without direct governmental control or interference. Many *Univisión* journalists see the CBS-*Telenoticias* project of bringing U.S.-style "objective" news to a hemispheric audience as the logical, desired result of their work pioneering Spanish language objective news on U.S. television. Several journalists at the Washington bureau of the *Noticiero* volunteered their hope that CBS would use its Latin America based reporters in both English and Spanish language news services, thereby legitimating Latin America as a topic for U.S. journalism.

For the journalists' imagined immigrant audience, Latin American reporting offers news of their *patria grande* of the pan-American hemisphere. Perhaps this is to be expected of a national news program produced for an audience made up of Latin American immigrants and their descendants. It seems simplistically misleading to conclude that *Univisión* would give prominence to news of "home," however. This is but one defining element of Latin American news in the *Noticiero.* "Home," too, is an imagined community and just the beginning of the analysis.

Univisión's coverage of Latin America constructs the intended audience as residents of a hemisphere, what the journalists call *"el continente americano,"* the American continent. The commercial imperative of Latino panethnicity has been broadened in the construction of pan-Americanism, the notion that the U.S. Hispanic market is one segment—albeit the wealthiest segment—of a hemispheric market that embraces Spanish speakers in North, Central, and South

America. The journalists assume that U.S. Latinos are interested in Latin American politics as well as the Latin American Olympic medal count and the deaths of Latin American actors and artists. General market national newscasts configure their global maps with the United States at the center, Asia at one periphery, and Europe on the other, along an east-west axis. The Latino-oriented news axis runs north-south, through the United States to Mexico and Central and South America.

This journalistic cartography prompts the *Noticiero Univisión* to have bureaus in Mexico City, Lima, Bogotá, and El Salvador.[21] In Latin American cities where it does not have correspondents, *Univisión* relies on *CNN en Español, Venevisión,* or *Televisa,* with which it has contracts for correspondent reports and video feeds. *Univisión* does not have correspondents in London, Paris, Tokyo, Beijing, or Moscow.

Latino national news production privileges news of the United States; the presumptive audience comprises U.S. Latinos. The *Noticiero Univisión* and the *Univisión* talk shows *Temas y Debates* (Topics and Debates), and *Cristina,* as well as the tabloid program *Primer Impacto* (First Impact) are seen throughout Latin America (by contractual arrangement and pirating). *Univisión* journalists insist, however, that their primary audience, "the one that counts," is the U.S. Latino audience.

By committing almost half their air time to Latin American news, the journalists of the *Noticiero* and the U.S. edition of CBS-*Telenoticias,* many of them immigrants themselves, are acknowledging the duality of immigrant life, especially recent immigrant life. Immigrants are between two countries, of two countries and not fully present in either. This is especially true of contemporary Latin American immigrants, many of whom, after settling in the United States, maintain close contact with their native countries, in many instances visiting frequently (Cornelius, 1992). Often, this national duality is evidenced in the selection of the lead story for a given day's program: A single lead story is not selected; two are. For example, on March 17, 1992, the *Noticiero* began,

> Jorge Ramos: Good evening. The primary elections today in Illinois and Michigan could decide which candidates will continue on to the finish line.

> Maria Elena Salinas: We will have extensive coverage of these elections later. But first, we go to Buenos Aires, Argentina, where this afternoon there were war-like scenes . . . The Israeli embassy in Buenos Aires suffered a dynamite explosion that demolished the building . . . Our correspondent Oswaldo Petrozino has this report from the scene.

This story was not motivated by a desire to cover news from home; there are relatively few Argentineans in the United States. From the point of view of a Mexican immigrant, the largest national origin Latino group (see Table 1.2), the

Noticiero Univisión offers little news from home. Of the 25 or so stories on each newscast, perhaps one or two will be about Mexico. Although Mexico is the most represented of Latin America countries on the *Noticiero* (22% of Latin America stories), the news is largely about the politics of the federal government in Mexico City, which may or may not have bearing on an immigrant's life or that of his or her family in Mexico.

The two other Latin American countries with large U.S. immigrant populations, Cuba and Puerto Rico, are the topic of relatively little news. Cuba makes up 3% of the *Noticiero*'s Latin America coverage; Cubans are about 10% of *Univisión*'s news audience. This is attributable to logistical difficulties and to the Cuban-born news managers' efforts to refute critics' "Cubanization" charge. Puerto Ricans constitute about 11% of the nation's Latino population; news about Puerto Rico in the period analyzed in the content analysis is negligible (although since the Goya boycott mentioned earlier, it has increased).

The notion of home for *Univisión* journalists is shaped by commercial and professional considerations. To illustrate, in the fall of 1991, journalists noticed that whenever the lead story of the West Coast edition was about Central America, *Noticiero* ratings increased. Salvadorans and Nicaraguans are among the fastest growing Latino immigrant groups in the United States; as recent immigrants, they are potential members of *Univisión*'s core mass audience.[22] The commercial imperative to maximize audience is interacting in this instance with the journalistic propensity to produce a good story. The civil wars and their aftermath in El Salvador and Nicaragua presented a continuing (almost daily) series of traditionally conceived newsworthy events to report on.

There is not a sizable Peruvian community in the United States; relative to other Latin American immigrant groups, the Colombian community is small. Yet the second largest group of Latin American stories (after Mexico) is news of those two countries.[23] The *Univisión* bureaus in Lima and Bogotá each provide the newscast two "wraps," or correspondent reports per week. This is not proportional to the relatively small Colombian and Peruvian immigrant communities in the United States, but rather to the newsworthiness of these countries' ongoing political upheavals. Here again, commercial and professional imperatives are mutually reinforcing: guerrilla insurgencies, illicit drug trafficking, and ongoing efforts to democratize these countries make for a steady supply of breaking and dramatic (and therefore presumably audience maximizing) news stories. Additionally, from an organizational point of view, the presence of the bureaus and the journalists and technicians who staff them makes for a steady supply of stories. In other words, the presence of a bureau "creates" news.

Moreover, *Univisión*'s emphasis on Latin American news is part of its larger panethnic, denationalizing project. The journalists believe that it is "natural," incontrovertible, that Latinos would be interested in news of *el continente americano,* the American continent—that a Mexican immigrant would be almost as interested in news of El Salvador as he or she would Mexican news. *Univisión* journalists believe the unifying force of this hemispheric identity is a bridge that blurs differences among the *Univisión* audience, thereby constructing a unitary "imagined community."

Daily news production is not generally organized around regional issues, however, but rather news of particular Latin American countries, most often "breaking" political and economic news regarding national governments. These stories are considered news by *Univisión* journalists because they relate events that happened yesterday or today or are likely to happen tomorrow, and because they involve high-ranking and/or powerful government officials. By incorporating mainstream forms such as the temporal frame and deference to government authorities, *Noticiero* journalists are able to preserve their objective narrative stance while presenting news of what—in the U.S. context—are unconventional datelines or points of origin for news. These daily news routines are largely unacknowledged by the journalists; they are habitual, workaday responses to the pressures of producing a daily news program. Another key *Noticiero* Latin American news routine is highly self-conscious, however.

Seventy four percent of the *Noticiero*'s Latin American news is about politics.[24] These political stories often inspire strong emotion among the *Noticiero* journalists, many of whom consider themselves to be political refugees. Cuban-born former news director Guillermo Martínez makes no secret of his disdain for Cuban leader Fidel Castro. Mexican-born coanchor Jorge Ramos left his native country because he was censored by the Mexican ruling party, the PRI. Melding U.S. Latino panethnic and U.S. journalistic objectivity considerations, political news about Mexico is routinely edited by Cuban Americans, and news about Cuba is edited by Mexican Americans. As Martínez explains, "I don't have an ax to grind in Mexico, and they [Mexican and Mexican American *Univisión* journalists] don't have an ax to grind in Cuba."[25] Since the spring of 1997 and the U.S. State Department and Cuban government's approval of CNN's Havana bureau, *Univisión* has been carrying reports from Cuba produced by CNN.

Unlike other U.S.-produced international news (including *Univisión*'s coverage of Europe, Africa, and Asia), the *Noticiero*'s reporting on Latin America is not primarily concerned with the United States. *Univisión* dedicates considerable resources to reporting U.S. military and diplomatic relations with various Latin American countries. Most often, however, events in Latin America do not need a U.S. angle to qualify as *Univisión* news. For example, the forced resignation of a member of the Argentinean cabinet is presented in much the same way as a U.S. presidential cabinet reshuffle. Summit meetings of Latin American presidents are covered in much the same way general market journalists cover, say, NATO meetings.

Both U.S. Spanish language television networks do regularly produce stories that highlight the interconnections of the U.S. and Latin American societies.

Examples include a report on how young Salvadorans deported from Los Angeles back to El Salvador for gang-related crimes reestablish gangs in San Salvador. A recurring theme is the dependence of Latin American countries on money sent from the United States by immigrants to their Latin American families and the threat to this monetary flow caused by accelerated deportations of unauthorized Latin American immigrants to the United States.

The largest number of stories highlighting this interconnectedness theme concern drug trafficking. The *Univisión* and CBS-*Telenoticias* Bogotá news bureaus produce continuing reports on Colombian *narcotráfico,* its effects on Colombian national politics, the ongoing Colombian civil war, and its effects on Colombian relations with the United States. These reports have a distinct Latino point of view: Latino journalists explicitly emphasize not only the flow of illicit drugs into the U.S. from Latin America, but also the demand side of this economic equation, that is, U.S. consumption and distribution of illegal drugs, something generally absent from general market stories about illegal drug trafficking. Asked why Latinos should be interested in coverage of Colombian decertification by the U.S. Congress, *Univisión* Washington, D.C., correspondent Armando Guzmán said, "Because, like me, they have teenage children."

Latino-oriented, nationally distributed news coverage of Mexico is the clearest example of this Latino charting of the globe. Mexico is not invariably considered to be "foreign" to the United States. The *Univisión* Mexico City bureau is one of the largest bureaus, having the same number of correspondents (two) as the Washington, D.C., bureau. Mexican politics and economics are continuing features of these newscasts. The *Noticiero* gave extensive, live coverage to the 1994 assassination of Partido Revolucionario Institucional (PRI) presidential candidate Luis Colosio, as well as to the devaluation of the *peso. Univisión* and the U.S. edition of *Telenoticias* have special election night coverage of elections in the United States and in Mexico.

The armed Zapatista insurgency in southern Mexico in 1994 and the continuing political and military instability that it has caused are topics for sustained reporting, as are crime and pollution in Mexico City and the precarious state of Mexican press freedom. Although consciousness of political cartography is heightened in the reporting on unauthorized Mexican immigration to the United States, the arbitrariness of the U.S.-Mexico border is also highlighted in this coverage. In many feature and arts stories, issues of nationhood are masked, seemingly irrelevant. A transnational comradeship is symbolically created and re-created each year when, to cite two examples, the *Noticiero* broadcasts consecutive stories about celebrations of Mexican independence day and commemorations of *la Virgen de Guadaloupe,* Mexico's patron saint, on both sides of the U.S.-Mexico border.

In its reporting on Latin America, the *Noticiero Univisión* creates a history, a collective memory for its imagined audience. Daily news stories offer U.S.

Latino immigrants a sense of where they came from. Hobsbawn (1983, pp. 9-12) writes of the intentionality of "invented traditions," common histories created by social institutions so as to legitimate themselves. In the case of *Univisión* news, the reporting on Latin America constructs a shared past for its audience of Latino immigrants, who are the core mass audience for the network. As has been argued throughout this book, however, the role of Latino news in the U.S. public sphere is more complicated than its economic function of helping legitimate the media enterprises. It also seeks to educate its imagined community and, in so doing, disseminate a panethnic, Latino identity.

NOTES

1. This chapter draws on A. Rodriguez (1996).

2. According to the February 1998 Hispanic Nielsen Television Index, the *Noticiero Univisión* is watched by 1.4 million Hispanic households; the U.S. edition of CBS-*Telenoticias,* distributed on the *Telemundo* network, is seen by about 150,000 Hispanic households. About 25 million U.S. households watch the three English language network newscasts (ABC, CBS, NBC), according to the Nielsen research.

3. For example, the news directors of both the *Noticiero Univisión* and CBS-*Telenoticias* are Cuban American.

4. About two thirds of the soundbites were of Mexicans or Mexican Americans, about 10% of Cubans or Cuban Americans, and an equal amount of Puerto Ricans, with the remainder of other Latin American nations. These numbers are subjective, based on my ability to identify various national origin accents (Rodriguez, 1993).

A quarter century ago, Leon Sigal (1973) discovered a similar pattern (also unknown by the journalists) amongst metro, foreign and national stories published by the *New York Times* and the *Washington Post.* Sigal's interpretation was that this avoided conflict amongst editors and reporters at the various news "desks."

5. Zablukovsky retired in 1998.

6. Many of the journalists who resigned formed the Hispanic Broadcasting Company, which evolved into *Telemundo.*

7. Godoy is today publisher of *VISTA,* a bilingual, nationally distributed monthly magazine, discussed in Chapter 7.

8. Diaz Balart, the brother of Congressman Lincoln Diaz Balart (R-FL), is currently an anchor with CBS news.

9. Today, *Televisa* distributes the ECO news service throughout Latin America and in the United States on *Univisión*'s premium cable channel, *Galavisión.*

10. Although the discussion here focuses on national newscasts, the major points are equally relevant for the analysis of local U.S. Spanish language television news in Chapter 6.

11. For a comparative analysis of the use of pronouns in Italian and U.S. television news, see Hallin and Mancini (1984).

12. This study thus joins the long list of those echoing the findings of Sigal (1973).

13. Although these figures are based on a 1993 content analysis, the findings are confirmed by a similar, week-long 1997 content analysis.

14. The content analysis shows that for instance, ABC spends 1.3% of its time on news about U.S. Latinos or U.S. Latino communities. See also Navarrete and Kamasaki (1994).

15. Latino stories are longer than other *Noticiero* stories, a mean of 143 seconds, compared to 26 seconds for other *Univisión* stories; they use roughly three times as many soundbites as other *Noticiero* stories; these soundbites are three times the average length of *Univisión* soundbites generally.

16. In 1998, Republican sponsors of the legislation joined with Democrats in restoring benefits to the roughly 1 million legal immigrants affected by the original laws.

17. In late 1998, measures to grant Salvadoran and Guatemalan immigrants temporary resident status were pending in Congress.

18. "[a]n open class structure, racial tolerance, economic mobility, the sanctity of individualism and the availability of the American dream" (Gray, 1989).

19. The racial categorization *Latino* is problematic. U.S. Latinos are multiracial: of African, native, Caucasian, or mixed-race heritage. See C. Rodríguez (1989).

20. Five percent of *Univisión* soundbites are of African Americans, whereas 10% of ABC's are. Similarly, 1% of *Univisión*'s soundbites are of Asian Americans, whereas ABC has 2% Asian American soundbites.

21. In 1992, when *Univisión* ownership changed, *Noticiero* news bureaus in Brazil, Argentina, and Chile were closed. At the same time, field producers in the network's domestic bureaus were laid off, and the network's weekly newsmagazine program *Portada* was canceled.

22. El Salvador stories make up 10% of *Univisión* stories; Nicaragua, 6%.

23. Peruvian and Colombian stories are each 12% of the total number.

24. Specifically, 29% about economics, 23% about war (including peace negotiations), 21% about government personnel reshuffles, 6% about human rights, 4% about elections, and 2% about labor strikes.

25. The animosity stems largely from the Mexican government's support of Cuban leader Fidel Castro. Most Cuban Americans identify themselves as political refugees from Castro's Cuba.

6

Local Latino News
Los Angeles and Miami

Local Latino news productions share many characteristics with the national newsmaking discussed in Chapter 5. The adaptation of general market journalism conventions to the presumed needs and interests of the Latino audience, an allegiance to journalistic objectivity, the prominence of Latin American news, and a fierce commitment to and promotion of Latino ethnoracial communities are clear continuities between nationally and locally distributed Latino news. Other commonalities include the prevalence of corporate sponsorship of Latino journalism (in major U.S. cities) and the service orientation of local Latino-oriented journalists. This chapter details the common structural factors—both economic and cultural—that characterize local U.S. Latino journalism and local Latino news audiences.[1]

This chapter also highlights profound differences among local Latino journalism enterprises, differences that are an expression of the political and social orientations that Latinos of varying national origins have adopted in the United States. In contrast with national Latino-oriented news, diversity within the ethnoracial group is not as easily masked in local news, largely because of predominant Latino settlement patterns, that is, Mexicans in the southwest, Cubans in south Florida, and Puerto Ricans in the New York City area. (This clear national origin mapping is being blurred by contemporary Latin American immigrant streams, however.)

Latino panethnicity—the notion of a unitary Hispanic culture that is the critical underpinning of national Latino media—has not been erased in local news productions, though generally it is muted and partially displaced by the particular concerns of local Latino marketing. The analysis below shows that the commercial ideal of *Hispanic U.S.A.* exists alongside, and sometimes in tension with, identities of specific national origin. The foundational differences among Latino groups—differences in U.S. socioeconomic status (detailed in Chapter 4)—are reflected in the political orientations of contemporary local Latino media.

To contextualize these differences, the media world of Los Angeles and Miami is detailed, as well as the demographic composition of the respective Latino populations. Local Latino media have a special social and political position within their respective cities. As fund raisers for victims of a Mexican natural disaster, sponsors of telethons for the poor during the Christmas season, initiators of public opinion polling as well as citizenship and voting drives, local Latino media are emblematic of the ethnoracial group, re-creating it with their distinct, widely amplified voices.

Local Latino news production features a self-conscious, sustained effort to produce service-oriented journalism. In general market journalism, this is commonly called "news you can use," and it focuses on the audience as consumers. Local Latino journalism often conceptualizes its audience as consumers. The Latino news audience is also understood as people in need of particular information about, and/or orientation to, dominant society institutions and practices. Contemporary local Latino-oriented journalism offers itself to Latino communities as an educator, a mediator in the social processes that transform Mexicans into Mexican Americans and Cubans into Cuban Americans.

The Latino journalism of Los Angeles and Miami brings the intraethnic diversity of Latinos into sharp relief. This diversity stems from differences in class, race, U.S. immigration histories, and the political ideologies of the two principal Latino groups in these cities, Mexican Americans and Cuban Americans. Cuban American median annual household income is about one quarter higher than that of the general Hispanic population; Mexican American median annual household income is just under that of the general Hispanic population (Bureau of the Census, 1997, Table 53, p. 52). Cubans came to the United States fleeing Fidel Castro's communist government. Mexicans came to the United States fleeing poverty. Cuban Americans tend to be registered Republicans. Most Mexican Americans vote Democratic.

So as not to lose sight of the profound similarities in Latino-oriented media, however, I first refer to a defining commonality that all local Latino-oriented media share. As Portes and Bach (1985) detail in their comparative study of Cuban and Mexican immigrants to the United States, Latinos are economic actors in a dual or split U.S. economy: an economy divided into the Anglo or white primary sector and the immigrant, largely Latino sector. Latino journalism, and Latino-oriented media generally, is part of the latter or secondary economic sphere of both Los Angeles and Miami, the largest of the majority Latino cities in the United States.

LOS ANGELES

Los Angeles is the nation's second-largest media market (after New York). Los Angeles is also the largest city of the Hispanic market,[2] with two full-time Spanish language television stations, two part-time Spanish language television stations, and 12 Spanish language radio stations. As mentioned in Chapter 4, KMEX-TV, Channel 34, owned and operated by *Univisión,* leads all Los Angeles television stations in the race for the 18-49 demographic group. Nine Los Angeles Spanish language radio stations are in the Arbitron top 40 for the Los Angeles area, with KLVE-AM consistently ranking as the first or second most listened to of 83 Los Angeles area radio stations. Los Angeles is home to one of the nation's largest-circulation daily Spanish language newspapers, *La Opinión* (The Opinion), as well as several bilingual and English language newspapers and magazines, which are examined in Chapter 7. Put another way, 35% of all advertising dollars spent in 1995 in the top 10 Hispanic market cities was spent in Los Angeles.[3] Another indicator of the market importance of the Los Angeles Latino audience is that most English language VHF television stations carry Spanish language translations of their newscasts on SAP, second audio channel.[4]

Some 5 million Latinos live in the Los Angeles metropolitan area. Within the city limits, about half of the population is of Latin American descent; surrounding areas all have significant Latino populations. Until recently, virtually all Los Angeles Latinos were Mexican and Mexican American. In the early 1980s, spurred by civil wars, hundreds of thousands of Central Americans migrated to southern California. Latino marketers estimate that although the Los Angeles area is still about 80% Mexican, immigrants from El Salvador now make up the next largest group, a community of roughly half a million people. They have been joined by other Central Americans, primarily from Nicaragua and Guatemala.

The great majority of Mexican immigration to the United States has historically and today been made up of unskilled, blue-collar workers. In the Los Angeles area (and throughout the southwest region of the United States), Mexican labor has been a source of low-wage labor in the larger, stratified labor market. Today, when three-generation Mexican American families are commonplace, the Los Angeles Latino-oriented media market is subdivided by age and by language use. Los Angeles Latino marketers, for example, refer to the "older Spanish speaking" market, meaning not elderly immigrants but rather *los abuelos* (the grandparents), longtime residents who may be bilingual but prefer Spanish language media.[5]

Los Angeles, since the late 19th century, has been a primary destination of Latin American migrants, and consequently immigration has been a central topic of Los Angeles Latino-oriented news. As Gerardo López, the editor of *La Opinión,* puts it, immigration is "our issue." In *La Opinión* news production, immigration is not a single issue. Rather, it is shorthand for a range of news topics that concern new immigrants as well as the larger Latino community, a community that continues to define itself and its place in Los Angeles society.

La Opinión, the Los Angeles Times, and the Hispanic Market

When Ignacio Lozano founded *La Opinión* in 1926, he didn't foresee a long life for the Spanish language daily, believing instead that Mexican immigration to the United States would soon cease, sure to end with the political turmoil Mexico was experiencing in the early decades of this century. Today, *La Opinión*'s audited circulation stands at 104,000, which, including a larger than general market pass-along rate,[6] permits the newspaper to claim a daily circulation of upwards of half a million copies. In *La Opinión*'s advertising and sales offices, English is the principal language; newsroom speech, however, is largely in Spanish, although several English language newspapers are scattered about: the *New York Times,* the *Wall Street Journal,* and, of course, the *Los Angeles Times.*

As discussed in Chapter 2, the *Los Angeles Times,* in the early decades of the century, regularly demonized Mexicans, when it covered them at all. Since the 1970s, the *Times* has appointed several Latinos to its reporting staff and editorial board, its Washington bureau has covered immigration issues extensively, and its Latin American bureaus are highly respected. Still, the journalistic cultures of *La Opinión* and the *Times* remained distant, while at the same time the two business offices were competing for a piece of Los Angeles's Hispanic market.

Beginning in the mid-1980s, *Los Angeles Times* management, taking note of the region's growing Latino population, began a concerted campaign to attract Latino readers. The *Times'* initial effort was called *Nuestro Tiempo* (Our Time), a monthly, bilingual supplement. *Nuestro Tiempo* was included in home and vendor delivery of the *Los Angeles Times* in majority Hispanic zip codes, and was available by mail to other *Times* subscribers. Its early promotional material, implicitly critical of *La Opinión,* proclaimed, "As Southern California's largest circulated Latino publication, *Nuestro Tiempo* means advertising success in any language."

The insert relied heavily on entertainment news: color photographs and light features about Spanish language television, music, and film celebrities. In 1988, in response to lower-than-expected advertising revenue, the format was changed to solely Spanish language. This strategy also failed to attract significant advertising support.

Two years later, the *Los Angeles Times* bought 50% of *La Opinión.* (*La Opinión* staffers are careful to call it an "investment" on the part of the *Times,* not a purchase.) This added a Spanish language daily to Times Mirror's media conglomerate, which today includes, in addition to the *Los Angeles Times*, the *Boston Globe*; Long Island, New York's *Newsday*; and various broadcast outlets. The *Times* and *La Opinión* editorial staffs remain separate, as do the printing and distribution operations. Members of the third generation of the Lozano family are in key ownership and management positions; Monica Lozano is associate publisher and executive editor of *La Opinión*; José Lozano is its president and publisher. The most salient aspects of the relationship between the two dailies are the joint marketing projects that have given the *Times* the niche it had been seeking in the Hispanic market.

A principal vehicle is *Para Ti* (For You), a tabloid-size, free weekly supplement to *La Opinión*. For much of 1996, *La Opinión's Para Ti* featured the theme *"La familia: Si se puede"* (The Family: Yes, We Can). Colorful, cartoon-illustrated issues include short articles, many of which read like public service announcements. For example, *"Seguridad Familiar"* (Family Security) contains items on poisonous and flammable household items, safety tips when using an automated teller machine, and an article on how to keep children from associating with gangs. The *Para Ti* format also includes celebrity news.

Both newspapers sell advertising; the *Los Angeles Times* distributes the supplement. *La Opinión* prints *Para Ti* and controls the editorial content. Marketing director Manny González is pleased with the results:

> When they [the *Los Angeles Times*] were publishing *Nuestro Tiempo*, they were our competitors . . . Now with *Para Ti*, the *Times* has introduced us to new advertisers, who never considered *La Opinión* in the past. For instance, Sears advertises in *Para Ti* [and the *Los Angeles Times*], but not in *La Opinión*.

Sharing the revenue of the Spanish language daily (and its new editorial products) is apparently not sufficient for the *Los Angeles Times* and its parent company, Times Mirror. The newspaper would like to reach a larger number of English speaking Latinos, Latinos who are the most attractive segment of the Los Angeles Hispanic market. A *Times*-commissioned study shows that only 20% of the Los Angeles area's Latino population reads the *Times*.

In 1997, *Times* publisher Mark Willes sparked a journalistic uproar when he proposed the creation of a separate news section for coverage of Latinos. The proposed Latino section would join other *Times* sections (e.g., Sports, Business, Metro) in an effort to lower (some would say eliminate) the walls between the business and editorial operations of the newspaper. The goal was to increase circulation and advertising revenue by creating permanent business units within each section of the *Times,* including the proposed Latino section.

Eighteen Latino reporters and editors were among 100 *Times* editorial staffers who sent a letter of protest to Willes, calling the idea "separate and unequal . . . It is offensive to create sections in this paper based solely on ethnicity." Many

journalists, general market as well as Latino-oriented, saw this as a direct affront
to their efforts to portray Latino communities as part of—not apart from—the
larger society (Aguilar, 1997; Peterson, 1997; Steingold, 1997; Turner, 1997).
Months earlier, *Times* editor (and former Metro columnist) Bill Boyarsky offered this insight into the *Times'* journalistic and commercial motivation:

> The people we are writing about [Los Angeles area Latinos] are striving to be mid-
> dle class, *a very American thing.* The challenge is to reach out to them in terms of
> what they are becoming. The suburbanization of the Latino middle class, that is the
> story. (as quoted in Rasky, 1997, p. 44, emphasis in original)

In late 1998, the *Times* announced that it would create an 11-member reporter
team headed by longtime editor Frank del Olmo to increase the newspaper's
coverage of Latinos and U.S.-Mexico affairs in all sections of the daily.

La Opinión and Latino Political Culture

According to market research commissioned by *La Opinión,* the average
household income of *La Opinión* readers is about $22,000. That is less than the
comparable figure for the Los Angeles general market of $38,400, and signifi-
cantly less than the Los Angeles Hispanic household income of $28,000 (Scar-
borough Research, 1995a). In other words, the readers of the Spanish language
daily are among the poorer members of the Los Angeles Hispanic market. Nonetheless, *La Opinión,* like other media, is sustained by advertising. Travel agencies are the single biggest advertisers, reflecting the transience of recent immigrant life. Also among the more frequent *La Opinión* advertisers are long
distance telephone companies and attorneys—personal injury, workers' com-
pensation, and immigration attorneys.

According to associate publisher Monica Lozano (drawing on *La Opinión*
market research), about half of the newspaper's readers are among Los Angeles's most recent immigrants; the other half

> came to the United States 12 to 20 years ago. They have kids born and educated
> here, and they own their own homes. They are bilingual but prefer to read in Span-
> ish, and they like the content they can't get anywhere else. (quoted in Rasky, 1997,
> p. 44)

These are working-class Latino families—secretaries, retail sales clerks, day
care providers, and construction workers—committed to building their lives
here, not in Mexico or El Salvador.

"Like everybody else . . . [our readers] care about crime, and drugs and housing," says *La Opinión* editor Gerardo López, "but recognizing that many are new

here, we go that extra step." Prominently displayed in López's office is a poster: "*Saber es poder*" (Knowledge is power). López is the first to say that *La Opinión* is produced "based on the interests of our readers." But he rejects the label *advocate*:

> I don't call it advocate. I think it is ethical for a journalist to have in his mind not only to sell newspapers, but to provide a source of information that is helpful to your community . . . We, as journalists are blessed with very powerful antennas . . . I think we are just being true to our journalistic mission.

Separately, Lozano said, "Everybody is busy talking about civic journalism, well, we've been doing it for years" (as quoted in Rasky, 1997, p. 44).

The Immigration Reform and Control Act (IRCA), signed by President Reagan in 1986, marked a critical turning point in Latino political culture, and Latino-oriented journalism. IRCA provided amnesty or legal residency for undocumented immigrants who could prove that they had lived in the United States for 7 years.[7] Nationally, some 3 million Latin American immigrants were "legalized," and after a waiting period became eligible for U.S. citizenship. The passage of IRCA was preceded by a decade of hearings and horse trading in Congress—a process that *La Opinión* reported in detail. "And we were still losing readers," remembers López.

After the bill's passage, *La Opinión* was flooded with calls from readers asking for details of the new law. In response, *La Opinión* produced a free 24-page brochure on IRCA's provisions that included phone numbers and information about agencies available to assist amnesty applicants. The first printing of the IRCA pamphlet was 500,000 copies (*La Opinión*'s circulation was about 70,000 at the time). A second printing of 250,000 copies soon followed. Over the next several months, as the specific regulations governing enforcement of the law were announced, *La Opinión* produced additional supplements. The *Los Angeles Times* then produced 1.5 million copies of a bilingual version of *La Opinión*'s IRCA brochures that were inserted in both newspapers. The public service campaign is the most elaborate, sustained example of López's "extra step."

La Opinión's journalistic service orientation has since been institutionalized in the newspaper's daily production. A series of stories on the 1996 general election "closed the circle for us," López said. This was the first presidential election in which new Latino citizens, those legalized as a result of the 1986 immigration law, could vote. *La Opinión* sponsored town meetings and special telephone lines, asking its readers to tell the newspaper "what they wanted to know." Based on that information, "that's how we did the elections," López said.

The Spanish language daily produced articles profiling the new voters, and in continuing sidebar stories to its regular election coverage, explained such U.S.

political concepts as caucuses, primaries, and the electoral college. Similarly, after the 1994 passage of California Proposition 187, which would have denied government benefits to undocumented immigrants, and 2 years later the passage of a federal welfare law that eliminated federal "safety net" benefits (food stamps, disability insurance) to legal immigrants, *La Opinión* produced special supplements on these new laws and on applying for citizenship.

In its routine coverage, *La Opinión* seeks to reflect its imagined audience back to itself though daily re-creation of the Los Angeles area Latino news agenda. To cite one day's coverage as an illustration, on June 10, 1996, the banner headline on *La Opinión*'s front page says, "*Crítica a política de México*" (Criticism of Mexican Policy). The story that followed featured Mexican residents of California border towns complaining that the Mexican government was not protecting citizens who were migrating to the United States. Other front page stories include Latino and African American higher education enrollment trends; the effect of the Helms-Burton legislation (which strengthened the U.S. embargo against Cuba) on hemispheric free trade; and a report on the possibility of double U.S.-Mexican nationality. An article about a Latino think tank study that showed that immigrants pay more taxes than they receive in government services is illustrated by an color graphic charting the relevant statistics. Another article by *La Opinión*'s Washington, D.C., bureau examines the Clinton White House's acquisition of the FBI files of prominent Republicans.

Only one of these stories, about the White House-FBI files controversy, is featured on the front page of the *Los Angeles Times*. The placement of a story on Mexico's budding economic recovery on the *Times'* front page reflects the acknowledged interconnectedness of the California and Mexican economies. The *Times* also ran front page articles on state government worker pay raises, Los Angeles city government politics, and a dispute before the Los Angeles county commissioners. Both newspapers have color sports photographs on their front pages: the *Times* one of basketball player Michael Jordan; *La Opinión* has a photo of a player in the U.S. major soccer league. The local story promoted on the front page of *La Opinión* is of a threatened public school teachers strike in a Latino (and African American) urban public school district; the *Times* front page promotes inside coverage on the death of a regional industrialist.

The contrast in this story selection is clear: Where *La Opinión* gives attention to news in which Latinos and Mexicans are the central players, the *Times* gives prominence to the actions of government officials and others of the Los Angeles area majority culture. Or, as editor Gerardo López summarizes the difference between the two Los Angeles newspapers, "We offer things of interest to Latino readers . . . the *Los Angeles Times* goes out and covers stories thinking of their readers."

Where the Metro section is in most major-city general market newspapers, *La Opinión* has "*Latino América*" (Latin America), made up largely of wire service reports (the majority of which are by the Associated Press and EFE, a Spanish news service) about the politics and economies of Central and South American countries. *La Opinión,* a local U.S. newspaper, also has bureaus in Mexico City and Tijuana, and regularly sends its reporters south to produce extensive features. In addition, *La Opinión* relies on informal, long-standing barter relationships with Mexican journalists for articles and photographs.

"*Espectáculos,*" or the entertainment section, uses wire services for its reports on Sean Connery and Julio Iglesias, while *La Opinión* writers provide regular coverage of the Latino/Latin American Los Angeles area music, theater, and gallery scene. Where major city general market business sections privilege news of Wall Street and transnational corporations, *Negocios* profiles successful small businesses on its front page; a popular column, "*Tecnología,*" explains how to maximize use of technology—from the telephone to accounting software.

Deportes (Sports) focuses more on boxing and World Cup soccer than general market sports sections do, but *La Opinión* also dedicates significant resources to covering the National Football League, as well as major league baseball, with its many Latino and Latin American players. Emblematic of this culturally hybrid sports journalism is the coverage of Mexican American Olympic boxing gold medalist Oscar de la Hoya. In special sections devoted to his June 1996 title fight against Mexican Julio Cesar Chavez, both Mexican and U.S. flags are colorfully displayed next to photographs of de la Hoya, while a graphic of a Mexican flag is placed next to Chavez. The coverage of the fight plays up a Mexican versus Mexican American rivalry, with contrasting hometown fan stories of Los Angeles and Ciudad Obregon, Mexico. (De la Hoya's nationalist celebrity has been furthered by glossy Latino-oriented magazine ads that feature him with a milk mustache, a U.S. flag draped around his shoulders.)

One final example of *La Opinión* journalism validates the journalists' assumptions about their audience. In 1995, the newspaper sponsored a public opinion poll with Los Angeles *Telemundo* affiliate KVEA-TV, Channel 52. Months after the passage of the anti-immigrant California Proposition 187, the poll asked Los Angeles area Latinos about the current Latino political climate. The respondents were 14% undocumented immigrants (who were promised confidentiality), 29% U.S. citizens, and 55% legal resident immigrants. They had a choice of answering questions in either English or Spanish.

When asked if they or a family member had been a "victim of racism," 83% of the respondents answered "yes." Another question asked respondents to choose among three "drastic actions, *acción drástica,*" that they favored in response to growing anti-Latino sentiment: "becoming citizens/voting"; "demonstrations"; and "strikes/civil disobedience." The majority, 57%, chose becoming citizens and voting.[8] This finding shows, in the journalists' view, that Latinos are law abiding people, who are, in the words of one *La Opinión* newsworker, "essentially conservative."

Although it is evident that *La Opinión*'s journalistic culture is different in many ways from that of general market U.S. journalism, this difference can also be exaggerated. *La Opinión* is a profit-oriented, advertiser-supported U.S. business. Further, the fundamental format of the Spanish language daily is that of traditional U.S. daily print journalism. Whether considered from the vantage point of the inverted pyramid that structures each hard news article, to the format of the editorial pages, and that of the celebrity-centered sports and entertainment sections, *La Opinión* is, in many defining dimensions, a product of the contemporary U.S. news industry. Within this framework, however, it offers its Los Angeles area imagined community a distinct prism through which to understand their world. Like the Latino Los Angeles television journalism examined below, *La Opinión* declines to step into the melting pot. At the same time, it demands and tries to facilitate an active role in the U.S. political culture for its audience.

Los Angeles Latino TV News:
The International Is Local

There are three Spanish language television stations in Los Angeles with local news operations. The market leader, KMEX-TV, Channel 34, is the flagship of the *Univisión* network. Established in 1962, KMEX was founded as, and to a great extent continues to be, a television station for Los Angeles Mexicans and Mexican Americans. It is, at this writing, the highest-rated station of all stations in the Los Angeles market, attracting more viewers than the English language networks' owned and operated stations (KCBS, KNBC, KABC), a fact KMEX trumpeted on billboards throughout Los Angeles (see Figure 6.1). KVEA-TV, Channel 52, is affiliated with the *Telemundo* network, and houses some of that networks' national production facilities. KWHY-TV, Channel 22, is an independent, non-network-affiliated Spanish language station. Its unusual institutional structure is one more indicator of the size of the Los Angeles Hispanic market.[9]

In many ways, local Latino-oriented television news is much like general market local television news: news, sports, and weather. There is, however, a central difference: In Latino-oriented news, the international is local. Latin American news is interwoven with reports about crime, the local city council, a major traffic accident, or a traditionally conceived human interest feature. This news selection reproduces a worldview that routinely crosses national boundaries in its definition of a local Latino world. Weather reports include that day's

Figure 6.1. KMEX Billboard
The KMEX 6:00 p.m. news team, from left to right: Bernardo Osuna, Andrea Kutyas, and Eduardo Quezada. Copyright © KMEX; used by permission.

high and low temperatures for Latin American capitals, as well as for the local city; the sports segment prominently includes Latin American soccer scores. Similarly, entertainment segments do not exclusively turn on Hollywood news; Mexico City is also reproduced as an entertainment capital. In local Latino newscasts, there is a special segment for Latin American news comprising quick headlines from that day's video feeds. Significant expenditures of these stations' limited resources (relative to the general market) are dedicated to news events outside the United States. Local Latino-oriented television news in Los Angeles, home to the largest number of Latinos in the United States, exemplifies these characteristics.

Los Angeles's Spanish language television stations all have bureaus (and/or regular freelancers) in Tijuana, Mexico. In addition, all have at least twice weekly correspondent reports from El Salvador. KMEX sent its own crew to cover President Clinton's 1997 visit to Latin America—in addition to broadcasting the *Univisión* network's extensive coverage. KVEA-TV, Channel 52, the Los Angeles *Telemundo* affiliate, produced a series on Los Angeles based gangs living in El Salvador. The Mexican consul general in Los Angeles is a regular local news actor. For Latino-oriented journalists, the cognitive map of the sprawling Los Angeles area spans eight counties in the United States and several Latin American countries.

Most Los Angeles Latino-oriented journalists have difficulty explaining why they pay so much attention to news from Latin America (as distinct from, and in addition to, news of Latin American immigrants in the United States). For these journalists, it is a taken-for-granted, unexamined aspect of their professional lives. Nonetheless, Sandra Thomas, news director for Los Angeles's KVEA, queried an audience focus group about the importance of Latin American news:

> We asked, "If there is a fire in your neighborhood [in the United States], and a fire in your hometown in Mexico or El Salvador, which news would you like to see first?" Women asked for the local one, thinking of their children. Men asked for their hometown . . . It's natural [to want to know about Latin America news]. It's interrelated. People who live in Los Angeles often go back in the winter. It's that feeling of not being away for good.

This characterization of a significant portion of the Los Angeles Latino news audience—that they are immigrants who have not yet, and may not ever, make an exclusive commitment to life in the United States—is commonly voiced by Los Angeles journalists. Most of the Spanish language television journalists, like their counterparts at *La Opinión,* believe that these "in-between" immigrants constitute a significant portion of their audience. Unlike many of their general market colleagues,[10] as evidenced by the news they produce, the presumptive audience of Latino television news does not consist of one-dimensional "illegal aliens." Rather, the imagined community for Los Angeles Latino journalism is diverse in terms of social status and political adaptation to the United States. This audience is also culturally unified by symbolic and material ties to Latin America, primarily Mexico and El Salvador.

Los Angeles's Spanish language television stations, especially KMEX-TV, Channel 34, the oldest and most firmly institutionalized, are Latino political and civic actors. In 1980, when the Spanish International Network (SIN) first began to create and promote a national Hispanic market and a nationwide Hispanic audience (see Chapter 3), KMEX, the network's owned and operated station in the nation's largest Hispanic market, took the lead on several fronts. Its *Destino 80* campaign, which was primarily aimed at encouraging Latinos to participate in the 1980 census, was the most elaborate. In the same period, as part of an effort to portray its audience as members of U.S. society, Channel 23 began live national broadcasts of the Tournament of Roses New Year's Day parade.[11] KMEX's telethons in response to the 1985 Mexico City earthquake raised hundreds of thousands of dollars.

Each election cycle, KMEX, through public service announcements, public affairs and news programming, and community events, conducts citizenship and voter registration campaigns. In the late 1990s, KMEX joined with other community organizations, including other Latino-oriented media, and Latino political groups (such as the Southwest Voter Registration Project and the League of United Latin American Citizens, LULAC) in an unprecedented citizenship, voter registration, and get-out-the-vote campaign.

Spurred to action by anti-immigrant legislation originating in both Sacramento and Washington, D.C., and by beatings and shootings of Latinos in the southwest,[12] Los Angeles Latinos participated in several large protest marches. Latino high school and college students rallied and organized walk-outs at their schools. These events and other public displays of Latino political discontent were reported by Los Angeles Latino news media. Further, in a sign of the alarm and anger with which Latino-oriented media responded to what Latino-oriented journalists commonly refer to as *la ola anti inmigrante* (the anti-immigrant wave), KMEX and KVEA broke with standard practice and editorialized against Proposition 187.

Latino-oriented broadcast media increased nonbroadcast community service oriented activities, such as establishing phone banks to address audience concerns about changing legislation. On the air, Latino attorneys were regularly featured on Spanish language television and radio news programs answering viewer inquiries about food stamp, disability, and educational program eligibility. KVEA-TV, Channel 52, for example, instituted a twice-weekly legal advocacy feature called *"52 a su lado"* (52 on your side).

From 1992 to 1996, there was a 30% increase in the number of California Latino voters. Put another way, Latinos cast 9.6% of all California votes in the presidential election of 1992. In 1996, Latino votes represented 13.2% of the state total. Clearly, with Propositions 187, 209, and 227 as well as Governor Pete Wilson's immigrant-bashing reelection campaign[13] and the federal immigration and welfare legislation of the mid-1990s, Latinos were highly motivated to become citizens and vote. Latino-oriented journalists' creation and dissemination of knowledge about the measures referred to above played a role in California's Latino political resurgence. Increased participation has not translated to election victories, however: Propositions 187, 209, and 227 were all approved despite opposition from the majority of California Latino voters.[14]

MIAMI

Sixty percent of the Miami population and 55% of surrounding Dade County is Hispanic. In the national Hispanic market, Miami is ranked number three, after Los Angeles and New York; it is home to the third largest population of Latinos.[15] This last statistic understates Miami Latinos' importance to Latino-oriented media and Latino politics generally. In the following passage from Joan Didion's (1987) *Miami,* the Spanish language evokes Miami's Latino political power:

> The sound of spoken Spanish was common in Miami, but it was also common in
> Los Angeles, and Houston and even in the cities of the northeast. What was un-

usual about Spanish in Miami was not that it was so often heard: in, say, Los Angeles, Spanish remained a language only barely registered by the Anglo population,
part of the ambient noise, the language spoken by the people who worked in the car
wash and came to trim the trees and cleared the table in the restaurants. In Miami,
Spanish was spoken by the people who ate in the restaurants, the people who
owned the cars and the trees, which made on the socioauditory scale, a considerable difference. (p. 63)

The volume and resonance of Miami Latino power derive from a particular
base: the wealth—monetary and cultural—of the city's Cuban American community. An understanding of the power of this wealth is enhanced when considered in comparison to that of other Latino groups.

The largest number of Mexican immigrants to the United States have historically been and are today unskilled and semiskilled workers. The largest portion
of Cuban immigrants, who settled in the Miami area in the early 1960s after Fidel Castro came to power, are white-collar and professional workers. In short,
"the history of the Cuban flow . . . has involved a substantial recomposition of
part of the Cuban bourgeoisie in South Florida" (Portes & Bach, 1985, p. 163).
Cuban Americans are nearly four times as likely to be self-employed as Mexican
Americans (Portes & Bach, 1985, p. 196). In 1980 with the Mariel boatlift, and
again in 1990s with the *balseros* (those who made the journey from Cuba in
homemade rafts), tens of thousands more Cuban migrants arrived in Miami.
These largely semiskilled workers were quickly absorbed into the enclave economy. In the decades since the initial 1960s migration from Cuba, Miami's verti-
cally integrated, ethnically enclosed economy has been key to the economic development of south Florida.

Nationally, 11% of all Hispanic-owned business are located in Miami. Los
Angeles, with four and a half times the Latino population, is home to 13% of
the nation's Hispanic-owned businesses (Hispanic Market Report, 1997). A
broader measure, average Hispanic household income, offers another sharp contrast: In Los Angeles it's $28,000; in Miami it's $42,300 (DRI/McGraw-Hill,
1994), higher than the national average for the general population. Predictably,
this economic base has found expression in the electoral arena.

Mexican Americans are represented on the Los Angeles city council and
county commissions and in southern California's delegations to national and
state legislatures. Miami Cuban Americans elected their first mayor in 1985; the
1997 mayoral race pitted two Cuban Americans against each other;[16] the region's congressional and legislative representatives are Cuban Americans. Dade
County and surrounding municipalities are also headed by Cuban Americans.
Perhaps as important, the presidents of several area banks, major retail estab-
lishments, public utilities, and universities are Cuban Americans.

Miami, increasingly Hispanic since large-scale Cuban immigration began in
the 1960s, is becoming less Cuban; Cubans and Cuban Americans now make up

less than half the Miami area Hispanic population. The Central American civil wars of the 1980s that have made Los Angeles less Mexican have also diluted the concentration of Cubans in Miami. In Los Angeles, the hundreds of thousands of recent Salvadoran immigrants are largely working class; the largest central American immigrant group in Miami is middle-class Nicaraguans who, like first-wave Miami Cubans, were fleeing a socialist government, the Sandinistas. Several South American national immigrant groups, principally Colombians, joined the Central American immigrants in the 1980s and 1990s. Domestic Hispanic immigration, largely from the New York City metropolitan area, has increased Miami's Puerto Rican population to about 9%.

The clout of Miami's Cuban Americans is not endangered, however. A 1994 accord between the Cuban and U.S. governments established a steady annual migration level of at least 20,000 Cubans, most of whom, it is assumed, will settle in south Florida. More important, as sociologist Alejandro Portes has said, Cubans are "the oldest, the most naturalized [as U.S. citizens, and therefore eligible to vote], the richest and the most solidarized" Latino group in Miami (as quoted in Navarro, 1997a). The political cohesiveness as well as the cultural identity of this prosperous community turns on its nationalism—Cuban nationalism.

Miami Cubans have their own lexicon with which they define themselves and their relation to the larger U.S. society. By and large, they don't refer to themselves as *Cuban American* though most are U.S. citizens or permanent legal residents, but rather as Cubans or *Cubanos*; their community is *el exilio* (the exile community), although the overwhelming majority have no intention of returning to Cuba to live. The larger society is *los americanos* (the Americans—the equivalent of Mexican Americans saying Anglos). Editor Barbara Gutiérrez, who came to the United States with her parents as a child, explains,

> [My parents left Cuba] because of an ideology. Because we were not going to be killed. My parents refused to bring up communist children . . . That's the bottom line of our tragedy . . . In any Cuban family gathering, Fidel [Castro] walks in, if not in the first 20 minutes, then certainly in the next 20 minutes. Because he is viewed as the one that changed everybody's lives.

The bitter tinge with which Gutiérrez tells the Cuban exile story is pervasive despite decades of acculturation and social integration. This is especially true among the politically active, including media workers.

The Miami Latino Media Market

Cuban Americans dominate the management ranks of Miami-based Latino-oriented media firms. Miami is headquarters for the two principal U.S. Spanish language television networks, *Univisión* and *Telemundo*. Six other Spanish language cable television networks (MTV-*Latino, Venevisión, Galavisión, CNN en Español*, CBS-*Telenoticias,* and GEMS) are also available in south Florida. *Editorial Televisa,* publisher of dozens of Spanish language magazines distributed throughout the hemisphere, is based in Miami, as are 12 Spanish language radio stations. In addition to two daily Spanish language newspapers, *El Nuevo Herald* and *Diario Las Americas,*[17] there are dozens of free weekly Spanish language newspapers called *periodiquitos* (little newspapers). The advertising-packed *periodiquitos* are published by small immigrant businesses and by politicians. The mayor of Hialeah, a city just north of Miami, published one, as does the chief executive of Dade County. *El Venezolano* is published by and for new Venezuelan immigrants, for example.

This extraordinary concentration of Latino-oriented, largely Spanish language media in a city of 1.3 million Hispanics has multiple, overlapping explanations. The first is that the largest identifiable (i.e., targetable) Latino population of Miami, Cuban Americans, is an attractive consumer group. In addition, this is a highly politicized community, one that values and thus routinely consumes political news, that is, daily journalism. Finally, Miami's position as the preeminent U.S. gateway city to Latin America is a critical context with which to understand the Miami Latino media market. South Florida's transportation networks to Latin America, by air and through the Miami port, are unrivaled. For the television networks, this makes possible frequent, inexpensive (relative to satellite transmission) air transport of taped programming. These transportation networks also make the Miami area a nexus for the distribution of Latin American goods in North America and the inverse, the distribution of U.S. goods to Latin America. Many Latin American companies have their U.S. headquarters in south Florida; Latin American elites have for decades vacationed and shopped in Miami. These add yet more affluence to the south Florida consumer market and a transnational, Miami-centered, Latino cultural market. In the words of Alberto Ibarguen, publisher of the *Miami Herald*, "Miami is so much smaller than Los Angeles or New York, the concentration [of Latinos] feels so much greater, you get the sense of a Latin city, a U.S. Latin city."

The *Miami Herald, El Miami Herald,* and Miami Political Culture

Sixteen years after the first wave of Cubans began settling in Miami, the *Miami Herald,* which is owned by Knight Ridder,[18] took professional notice of the Cuban community. Its initial effort was a column; 2 years later, *El Miami Herald* began publication. This began as a one-page Spanish language insert and was expanded to as many as 18 pages. *El Miami Herald* was essentially a translation of the *Miami Herald.* It had just four Spanish language journalists on its staff.

Current staffers remember that whenever there were budget cuts, *El Miami Herald* shrunk in size and personnel. Most significant, *El Miami Herald* never had its own editorial board; its editorial and opinion columns were Spanish language translations of *Miami Herald* editorials.

In the late 1970s, *El Miami Herald* editorialized (in a translation of the main newspaper's editorial) that, although perhaps a bit extreme, Fidel Castro had brought free health care and education to the Cuban population, and for this should be commended. Editor Barbara Gutiérrez remembers this as a turning point for Miami's Cuban community, "We were not forgiven for that [the editorials] . . . some [in the Cuban community] still hold it against us . . . We are talking about a community that was extremely conservative by American standards because of what they had gone through, the revolution, exile."

Compounding this, just a few years later, the *Miami Herald,* and so *El Miami Herald* in translation, editorialized against the Nicaraguan *contras* (*contrarevolucionarios,* or counterrevolutionaries), the U.S.-trained and -financed soldiers President Reagan called "freedom fighters." During this period, Cuban Americans were organizing well-attended marches in Miami in support of the *contras* and the overthrow of the socialist Sandinista Liberation Front. Chanting reverberated in Little Havana, the center of Miami's Cuban community: *"Nicaragua Hoy! Cuba Mañana!"* (Today Nicaragua! Tomorrow Cuba!).

The Cuban American National Foundation (CANF), the most vocal and visible political organization of the *exilio,* responded to the editorials by organizing a boycott of the *Herald,* buying advertisements on the backs of city buses, and distributing leaflets and bumper stickers that proclaimed, "We don't believe the *Miami Herald.*" *Herald* employees received death threats, and *Herald* vending machines were filled with excrement. CANF and its president, Jorge Mas Canosa, denied involvement with the unlawful protests. These symbolic fisticuffs between Miami's Cuban community and its newspaper of record occurred in the overheated, extralegal context of efforts by the extremist wing of the Cuban *exilio* to overthrow Cuban president Fidel Castro.

For many Cuban Americans, John Fitzgerald Kennedy is not a hero. To the contrary, he is, even today, regularly vilified as the man responsible for the defeat of Cuban American forces at the Bay of Pigs in 1961.[19] Soon after Castro's ascent to power in 1959, Cuban American, south-Florida-based paramilitary groups began organizing and training with the U.S. Central Intelligence Agency (CIA) to remove Castro from power (Hersch, 1997, p. 378). A member of one of these groups was convicted in 1985 on 71 counts related to a series of bombings that took place in New York City and Miami in the late 1970s and early 1980s.

Media outlets that were bombed included *El Diario-La Prensa,* a New York daily, and *Réplica,* a Miami Spanish language newspaper. In 1976, Emilio Milan lost his legs in a bombing after suggesting on WQBA, a Miami Spanish language radio station whose call letters are pronounced *Cuba,* that the bombings were counterproductive and that dialogue with Castro was a better alternative. Omega 7 claimed credit for many of these acts in broadcasts on Miami Spanish language radio stations (Didion, 1987; Hersch, 1997). One of these radio stations, at the time the highest rated of all radio stations in the city, was charged with inciting a riot (Ynclan, 1984). This was the political context that nourished the tension between the *Miami Herald, El Miami Herald,* and parts of Miami's Cuban community, as editor Barbara Gutiérrez explains:

> [It was] basically a clash of cultures . . . Cubans after the Bay of Pigs have always felt betrayed by the U.S. . . . Some felt they had to take things in their own hands. . . . So there were movements [in Miami] that would have been considered terrorist by anyone, except Cubans.

In 1980, tensions between this well-organized, high-profile segment of the Cuban community and the larger Miami society were further strained by the arrival of tens of thousands of Cuban immigrants, the wave of immigration called the "Mariel boatlift." Also in 1980, one of Miami's black neighborhoods, Liberty City, was the site of several days of rioting, a reaction to allegations of police misconduct.

The *Miami Herald*'s response to this civil unrest was to increase its coverage of its "minority" communities. One example was a 1983 story in the Sunday magazine that was headlined "The Cubans: They are ten of the most powerful men in Miami. Half the population doesn't know it." The story was written by *Miami Herald* Cuban American reporter and columnist Guillermo Martínez.[20] The intent of the article, writes Martínez, was to bridge the social chasm between Cubans and the rest of Miami, as this excerpt shows:

> . . . to challenge the widespread assumption that Miami's Cubans are not really Americans, that they are a foreign presence here, an exile community that is trying to turn south Florida into north Cuba . . . The top ten are not separatists; they have achieved success in the most traditional ways. They are solid bedrock citizens, hardworking humanitarians who are role models for a community that seems determined to assimilate itself into American society. (as quoted in Didion, 1987, p. 56)

This embrace of the melting pot, although clearly heartfelt, does not address the secondary status accorded *El Miami Herald* by the *Miami Herald* and Knight Ridder.

El Nuevo Herald

In 1987, Knight Ridder and the *Miami Herald* decided to start fresh with *El Nuevo Herald.* The New Herald was intended to leave behind the *Herald*'s sometimes rocky relationship with Miami's Cuban community. With the national Hispanic market flourishing and Latinos making up half the Miami area population, the renewed initiative made sense from both journalistic and marketing viewpoints. The break with *El Miami Herald* journalistic practices was not a complete one, however.

For most of its existence, *El Nuevo Herald* was a supplement to the *Miami Herald,* folded inside about 40% of the home-delivered English language newspapers. *El Nuevo* was also available in vending machines located in Latino neighborhoods and downtown Miami. This distribution system, *El Nuevo* journalists and marketers readily acknowledge, left them with a less-than-clear idea of who the newspaper's readership was. Their consensus was that in some households, *El Nuevo* was thrown away, unopened. In other, multigenerational households, they speculated, the children read the *Miami Herald,* the grandparents *El Nuevo,* and the parents, staffers hoped, looked through both newspapers.

In mid-1998, *El Nuevo Herald* became available to subscribers and vendors independently. Early audits put weekday circulation at 80,000; Sunday *El Nuevo* circulation is 90,000. Market research commissioned by *El Nuevo Herald* emphasizes that the Spanish language daily reaches more of Dade County's Hispanic college graduates, with household incomes of $35,000 and above, than Spanish language television and radio (Scarborough Research, 1995b). The bottom line, *El Nuevo* marketing director Bob Oliva tells potential advertisers, is "if you don't advertise in the Miami Hispanic market, you are missing half the market."

El Nuevo Herald content is about 30% translations of the *Miami Herald,* but its editorial and opinion pages are independent. The *Miami Herald* has about five times the staff of *El Nuevo.* The Spanish language daily has its own staff of about 80, which includes 19 reporters who write only for *El Nuevo.* Notably, when Knight Ridder was laying off staff and otherwise cutting costs in 1991 at its other newspapers (including the *Miami Herald*), it increased *El Nuevo*'s resources.

A comparison of the front pages of the *Miami Herald* and *El Nuevo Herald* on Thursday, February 6, 1997, illustrates how, despite joint ownership and overlapping news production, the two south Florida dailies each have distinct conceptualizations of who their audience is and what news is. There are six stories on each front page. The lead article in the English language *Herald* is about a new plan by the Miami police chief to control crime in the city. Two other front page *Herald* stories concern the O. J. Simpson verdict.

The *El Nuevo* lead is about a White House plan to encourage a change in the control of the Cuban government. The Miami police chief story is *El Nuevo*'s secondary lead. Three other *El Nuevo* front page stories concern Latin American politics: disarmament in Nicaragua; a coup in Ecuador; and plans to sell Cuban *pesos* on the open market. A photograph of O. J. Simpson directs readers to stories on page 9. Each newspaper features large color photographs next to the crime prevention stories. The *Miami Herald*'s photograph is of an African American child and mother, both crime victims. *El Nuevo Herald*'s photo is of young Latinos unveiling an anticrime sculpture at police headquarters. The Spanish language daily privileges news about Latin America and Latinos, including, but not limited to, Latino immigrants.

Mindful that half its readers and potential readers are not Cuban and that many are recent immigrants, Miami's largest Spanish language daily intersperses articles about municipal politics (in which the major actors are Cuban Americans) with service-oriented pieces that include concrete information about changing federal immigration laws. *El Nuevo,* like *La Opinión,* has an immigration hotline for its readers.

Although all the journalists whose work is cited here say they practice journalistic objectivity, "the other side" of stories about Fidel Castro and the Cuban government is routinely absent. Part of the explanation for this is operational and organizational. Local Miami news organizations, like most other U.S. news organizations, have not been permitted to open bureaus in Cuba. The *Univisión* network, which is carried in Miami, regularly airs *CNN en Español* reports from Cuba. The consequence of this lack of access, and in the more diffuse influence of highly organized anti-Castro groups, is that reporting critical of Cuba is rarely rebutted in Miami.

Local Miami news does include some voices calling for dialogue with Castro, but they are not frequently heard. The most prominent example is Liz Balmaseda of the *Miami Herald,* whose column is occasionally translated in the *Nuevo Herald.* Many observers of Miami politics point out that the extremist views of the Cuban American National Foundation and other *exilio* organizations have never been representative of the Cuban American community, but rather only of a segment of the generation who immigrated to the United States as adults in the 1960s. As these people age, their voices are growing muted and those of a younger, more pluralistic Cuban American generation are taking their place (Torres, 1997).

A comparison of the two leading U.S. Spanish language dailies shows as many similarities as differences. Like *La Opinión, El Nuevo Herald* is a daily newspaper purposefully created to meet the perceived journalistic and marketing needs of an ethnoracial Latino group. Accordingly, the similarities between the two U.S. Spanish language daily newspapers are many: Both have daily sections called "*América Latina,*" in the place where most big city general market dailies have a metro or city/regional section; both the Miami and Los Angeles daily Spanish language newspapers' sports and entertainment coverage feature articles about Latin American and Latino celebrities, along with stories about Hollywood stars and National Football League heroes.

The front page of each U.S. metropolitan Spanish language newspaper includes stories where the principal news actors are Latinos and/or Latin Americans and where the journalistic event is understood to be of particular interest to Latino communities. The international coverage of the two newspapers reflects the particular national origin of their respective readers: *El Nuevo*'s principal focus is on Cuba, Colombia, and Nicaragua; *La Opinión* privileges news of Mexico and El Salvador. Both newspapers reprint stories from major Latin American dailies; the editors of both newspapers call these arrangements "partnerships."

The differences in the content of *El Nuevo Herald* and *La Opinión* illustrate the distinctive political, social, and economic orientations of their respective imagined audiences. Most striking (to this out-of-town visitor) is *El Nuevo*'s weekly, tabloid size, color, regional real estate section. (*La Opinión* has a real estate section in the classified advertisements.) This sign that the *El Nuevo* targeted audience has capital to invest is complemented by advertisements in the body of the newspaper from firms traditionally associated with immigrant cultures: long distance telephone services and English language classes.

Miami Latino Television News

Miami general market media, to perhaps a larger degree than the media of other majority Latino cities (e.g., Los Angeles, San Antonio), incorporates Latino-oriented news topics into its daily English language coverage. This reflection of the middle-class status and political power of many Miami Latinos is symbolized by the Cuban American ethnic identity of several general market weekday news anchors and general assignment reporters.

Further, Miami general market television stations have—at their initiative—entered into partnerships with Miami Spanish language television journalists. In these informal video bartering arrangements, the Spanish language stations give video of events in the Latino community that the English language stations did not cover (and vice versa). These kinds of journalistic arrangements reflect the prominence of Cuban Americans in the regional power structure and somewhat blunt what Entman (1990) calls the "modern racism" of much of general market journalism about racial minority communities. As in other cities, however, coverage of Latino-oriented journalistic concerns is not a routine part of Miami English language television news.

Robert Vizcón, news director of Channel 51, *Telemundo*'s Miami affiliate, summarizes his news agenda: "We're into empowerment issues." Targeting a recent immigrant audience, WSCV-TV each week features a segment called *"Cuando yo llegué"* (When I Arrived) and *"Lo mejor de lo nuestro"* (The Best of Us) profiling successful immigrant business people and community leaders. Vizcón explains the motivation for these features: "We want to show immigrants that 'you can do it too. The country is full of opportunities and it's only up to you to get where you want to go.' "

In a more directly service-oriented vein, Channel 51, in addition to its daily reporting, sponsored an attorney-staffed telephone hotline to answer questions about the federal government's immigrant visa lottery and cuts in benefits to legal residents.

We [and *Univisión*'s Channel 23] are running five-part series [during sweeps week] on the SSI [Social Security Insurance] mess because that's what our public wants. They need to know that even if you are a legal resident, you could lose— that you have to become a citizen now.

This unabashed journalistic advocacy of Latino participation in U.S. electoral politics is, in the case of Miami Latinos, enhanced and encouraged by Latino legislative power.

Univisión's WLTV-TV, Channel 23, has, since its founding in 1971, taken its commitment to south Florida's Cuban community beyond daily news coverage. In addition to telethons for the poor and the sponsorship of musical events, Channel 23 journalists, to a degree unusual for broadcasters (regardless of language), seek to create and re-create the collective memory of Cuban Americans. Channel 23's special projects unit produced documentaries and special series on the 30th anniversary of the Cuban Revolution (Castro's ascent to power), the 25th anniversary of the Bay of Pigs and the Cuban missile crisis, and the 10th anniversary of the Mariel boatlift.[21]

More recently, Channel 23 canceled all regularly scheduled programming (and so advertising revenue) in February 1996 when a plane piloted by Cuban Americans (belonging to *Hermanos al Rescate,* Brothers to the Rescue, a self-described humanitarian group) was shot down by the Cuban government. On the first anniversary of that shooting (to the minute) both Channel 23 and Channel 51, as well as Miami's Spanish language radio stations, observed a minute of silence. Channel 23 also provided live coverage of the first anniversary memorial service for the pilots; the funeral of Jorge Mas Canosa, founder of the Cuban American National Foundation; and the Pope's 1998 visit to Cuba (this in addition to the network *Univisión* coverage). These journalistic productions were marked as special, ritual commemorations of key events in the Cuban American community.

As early as 1983, Channel 23 was the highest rated of all Miami television stations. Those measurements were taken by the Arbitron company (better known and respected for its radio ratings services), however, and were discounted by most advertisers. Today, considering both Spanish language network affiliates together, Spanish language television accounts for about 70% of the

Miami market. Channel 23 regularly bests Miami's general market stations in several key demographic groups and time periods, including early prime (*Cristina* vs. *Oprah*) and the news block (network and local), echoing the performance of the Los Angeles-owned and -operated *Univisión* affiliate.

Miami Spanish language television's success—like that of Los Angeles's Spanish language television stations—has come at the expense of Miami's English language stations. The general market stations have complained directly to the A. C. Nielsen Company, saying that the Miami ratings sample includes an excessive number of monolingual Spanish households. The English language stations allege that Nielsen is "double dipping," combining the Hispanics in its National Hispanic Sample Index, NHSI (see Chapter 4) with its standard sample. Bob Leider, vice president and general manager of Sunbeam Television's Fox affiliate, told an interviewer, "The stations are taking action. We're fed up . . . We want a sample geographically spread . . . and we want them to be bilingual families" (as quoted in Brodesser, 1997, p. 15).

Jack Loftus, a Nielsen representative, says the company is standing by its data and its methodology: "They claim we are measuring the wrong Hispanics. As Miami becomes more Hispanic, their screams will become a lot louder" (Brodesser, 1997).

Despite all the differences between Miami and Los Angeles Spanish language news media, differences that stem from the distinct class and U.S. immigration histories of the respective Hispanic audiences, it is worth noting a fundamental commonality. All these newsmaking enterprises rely on their imagined audience's Latino ethnoracial identity, whether that target audience is longtime residents or recent immigrants, to motivate and define the journalism.

NOTES

1. Due to space constraints, this book does not consider the thriving Latino-oriented media of New York, Chicago, and San Antonio (and many other U.S. cities). These cities all have local, Spanish language television newsrooms, as well as locally produced daily and weekly bilingual and Spanish language newspapers. New York's Spanish language daily, *El Diario-La Prensa* (circulation approximately 50,000), for example, has been publishing continuously since 1913 under a variety of ownership arrangements.

2. The sprawling Los Angeles "designated market area" (DMA) includes Los Angeles County, Orange County, Santa Barbara County, and Ventura County, as well as parts of Kern, Riverside, and San Diego counties.

3. Data for this market profile are drawn from Tiegel (1995) and *Hispanic Business*'s (1997) "Annual Hispanic Market Report."

4. SAP is available, for an extra fee, from local cable services. The size of this audience is not measured.

5. Market research commissioned by Spanish language newspapers, similar to that by English language newspapers, shows that newspaper readership, "skews older," that is, newspaper readers tend to be middle-age and older adults.

6. *Pass-along circulation* refers to the (unaudited) reading of print media by those who did not personally purchase it, for example, coworkers, public transportation users, and family members.

7. IRCA also established penalties or sanctions for employers who hired undocumented workers, as well as a "guest worker" provision for temporary immigrant labor.

8. Thirty-three percent chose demonstrations; 4% chose strike/civil disobedience.

9. KWHY was formerly affiliated with *Galavisión, Univisión*'s cable network.

10. See studies of Latino portrayals in general market journalism cited in Chapter 1.

11. The Tournament of Roses parade live broadcast has become a *Univisión* network standard.

12. One example that gained particular attention was the shooting death of a young U.S.-citizen Latino shepherd by a Latino Marine assisting the Border Patrol near Riverside, California. No convictions resulted from this incident. Without acknowledging responsibility or guilt, the Justice Department (parent agency of the Border Patrol) settled with the family for $1.9 million. In 1998, a scathing Congressional report recommended a thorough revamping of the relationship between U.S. military and Immigration and Nationalization Service (INS) agents along the border (see Paulsen, 1998).

13. Governor Wilson's advocacy of Proposition 187 was the centerpiece of his 1994 reelection campaign—a tactic that propelled the former U.S. senator from a large deficit in the polls to a comfortable winning margin. According to Wilson's pollster, more than 90% of the respondents knew Wilson's position on 187, more than those who could identify Sacramento as the state capital (Cornelius, 1995).

14. In 1998, the first Latino California lieutenant governor was elected.

15. In the U.S. general media market, Miami is considered a midsize, not a major market.

16. A grand jury investigation of the 1997 Miami mayoral race found evidence of dead voters, fraudulent addresses, and manipulation of elderly voters by campaign volunteers (Navarro, 1997a). The courts voided this election, and Cuban American Joe Carrollo was reinstated as mayor.

17. *Diario Las Americas,* one of the few Latino-owned, Latino-oriented media outlets in the country, is a fiercely anti-Castro advocacy newspaper deserving of separate analysis.

18. Knight Ridder also owns, among other media properties, the *Philadelphia Inquirer* and the *San Jose Mercury News.* In 1995, Knight Ridder began publishing a Spanish language weekly newspaper in northern California.

19. Recently published investigations reveal that "the necessity of Castro's death [was, for JFK] . . . a presidential obsession" (Hersch, 1997, pp. 3; see also Weiner, 1998).

20. From 1987 to 1992, Martínez was vice president for news of *Univisión.* At this writing, he is developing news programming for *Venevisión,* the Venezuelan media company.

21. These programs were produced by Maria López, currently executive producer of *Univisión*'s "tabloid TV" daily program *Primer Impacto.*

7

Bilingual and English Language Media

Bilingual and English language Latino-oriented media, mostly magazines but also electronic media, represent the latest efforts to re-create the Hispanic audience as a viable commercial product. This isn't an entirely new concept. Several of the earliest Latino-oriented newspapers were Spanish-English bilingual, and in at least one case, Spanish-English-French trilingual. These 19th-century newspapers were published by and for merchants in the ports of the Gulf of Mexico and the Caribbean Sea that linked the United States and Latin America. Like today's bilingual and English language Latino news, the journalism produced in these early newspapers targeted a specialized audience, and the newspapers were run as businesses (Wilson & Gutiérrez, 1995, pp. 177-181).

Although sharing these key characteristics, today's bilingual and English language Latino journalism is also vastly different from its antecedents. The contemporary media are largely sustained not by international economic transactions but by domestic ones, namely the U.S. Hispanic market. Although much of today's bilingual and English language Latino audiences are social and economic elites, many are not. Bilingual and English language Latino audiences represent an emergent, yet-to-be-firmly-institutionalized reconceptualization of the Hispanic market and Latino-oriented journalism. The English language is the primary tool used to subdivide the Hispanic audience and increase its value. The English language in this context is proxy for class; Hispanic English language and bilingual media are targeting a more valuable middle-class Hispanic audience. The clearly defined panethnic conceptualization of Hispanic audience, the nexus of which is the Spanish language, is being challenged. Bilingual and English language Hispanic media represent a potential paradigm change in notions of the Hispanic audience.[1]

Today, U.S. Spanish language broadcasting (radio as well as television) dominates the Hispanic market, accounting for 90% of Hispanic market advertising. The resiliency of the commercial and cultural belief that Latinos exclusively speak Spanish is explained by several factors. The overarching cultural conflation of ethnicity, race, and the "foreign" Spanish language has been reinforced in general market media, in both journalistic and fictional productions. These media spotlights have been trained on the most recent Latin American immigrants to the United States, typically monolingual Spanish speakers.

Latino-oriented Spanish language media marketers also emphasize the Spanish language as the central identifying characteristic of the Hispanic audience, most notably in the widely distributed Hispanic Nielsen ratings. From a sociological perspective, more than half of current Latin American immigrants arrived in the United States since 1980. Like 19th-century Western European immigrants, Latinos need time, usually a generation or two, to improve their English language skills.

The notion that an English language and/or bilingual Hispanic audience exists is a sharp departure from established Hispanic audiencemaking. From a marketing point of view, however, it is clearly appealing: Segmenting Hispanics by language use has the potential of producing a more tightly defined audience, one that is targetable not only by ethnoracial identity but also by class. This English speaking and bilingual segment of Hispanics is more educated and has more disposable income, and so is more attractive to advertisers.

Like their Spanish language Hispanic market counterparts, English language and bilingual marketers have assembled numbers to validate their claims. The key figures for English/bilingual audience researchers are reported in the 1990 census. The language use section of the census survey shows that more than half (54%) of Latinos self-reported that they speak English and Spanish "very well"; 20% said they spoke both English and Spanish "well." Eight percent of the Hispanic Census Bureau respondents reported they spoke no Spanish—26% stated they don't speak English at all or "not well." In sum, about three quarters of Latinos are bilingual.

From a media marketing or audiencemaking perspective, the most important research is that which correlates English language use with higher incomes. All the Latino-oriented English and bilingual media firms discussed in this chapter have commissioned market research that demonstrates that middle-class Latinos tend to be bilingual or English dominant. A more disinterested source, the Census Bureau, reports that the higher the U.S. educational attainment (indicator of English language usage), the higher the annual income of U.S. Hispanics. Efforts to reach middle-class Latinos through the general market—like any effort to reach a niche audience through traditional means—are by definition expensive and inefficient. In marketing terms, trying to target middle-class Latinos with advertising on say, CBS, would generate costly "excess eyeballs."

Broad demographic statistics buttress a reinterpretation of what *Hispanic* means linguistically, socially, and economically, and thus in terms of audience construction. The Hispanic population growth promoted by Spanish language media marketers also applies to the more acculturated segments of the Hispanic market. In other words, not only has the Spanish monolingual, relatively poor Latino population been growing, so has the population of wealthier, bilingual, and English-dominant Latinos. One widely circulated study shows that in the 1980s, the number of middle-class Latinos in southern California grew three and a half times faster than poor Latinos; that fully half of southern California Latinos own homes; and that just under half have annual average household incomes of between $30,000 and $120,000 (G. Rodriguez, 1996). Taken together, these numbers suggest the complexity of contemporary Latino language use and, more broadly, cultural patterns.

From a political cultural perspective, studies show that like previous U.S. immigrant groups, Latin American immigrants have learned and today continue to learn English (Gonzáles, 1998). Further, research suggests that portions of Latino communities, primarily those in the middle and upper ranges of the socioeconomic scale, are English dominant, that is, they use English in most aspects of their daily life. Of this group, some have retained Spanish as a second language, and some Latinos don't use the Spanish language at all.

Marketers and other cultural commentators refer to English-Spanish bilingualism as "retro-acculturation," a reaffirmation of Latino ethnicity that simultaneously embraces a U.S. national identity. Although this latter Hispanic audience is difficult to quantify, its existence is abundantly supported by anecdotal evidence.

In the context of U.S. publishing, English language and bilingual Latino journalism is an element of the growth of specialized magazines that has occurred in the U.S. media market in the past several decades. These tightly targeted publications, like their cable television counterparts, are made possible by the proliferation of audience measurement technologies. Whether products of the Hispanic market or of the general market (e.g., *Vegetarian Times, Family PC*), these niche market media turn on the specification of their audiences (Barnes & Thomson, 1994).

For bilingual and English language Hispanic media, the core of audience construction is the use of the English language by Latinos. In the sociolinguistic and historical literature, adoption of the dominant society language has been seen as a sign of assimilation, the absorption of an ethnic minority group into the larger society (Fishman, 1972, 1989). In sharp contrast, the analysis that follows shows that, in the case of contemporary English language and bilingual Latino-oriented media production, the embrace of the English language is not equated with the erasure of these media's distinct ethnoracial identity.

After a brief introduction to bilingual Hispanic media, the balance of this chapter examines particular examples of English language and bilingual Latino-oriented journalism. Throughout, special focus is given to the production of the audience for these newest forms of Hispanic media.

BILINGUAL HISPANIC MEDIA

Bilingual Hispanic media are trying to create a numerically significant Hispanic middle-class audience, an audience that its producers and marketers hope will eventually rival the Spanish language Hispanic audience. Although the percentages vary by state, according to the 1993 DRI/McGraw-Hill Hispanic Language Use Survey (based on 1990 Census data), the majority of Hispanics are bilingual. The 1996 National Latino Voter Survey (de la Garza et al., 1996) reports that 60% of Hispanics were born in the United States, and just 30% are "Spanish dependent," that is, exclusively use the Spanish language. Strategy Research Corporation, in its 1998 Hispanic market study (Freeman, 1998), headlines the finding that the number of Hispanics watching English language television is steadily rising, and that on an average day Hispanics use Spanish language media for 4 hours a day and English language media for 4 hours a day.

The bilingual sector of U.S. Hispanic media industries remains small, however. This despite bilingual media's potential: It offers the possibility of large audiences, of both Spanish and English speaking Hispanics. Nonetheless, from a marketing/audience research point of view, the bilingual Hispanic audience is not currently efficiently identifiable, measurable, or targetable as compared to either the English or the Spanish language Hispanic audience.

The core of the elusive bilingual Hispanic audience is the hybridity (García Canclini, 1995; Hall, 1993) of U.S. Latino public culture. Bilingual Hispanic media construct an ethnicity that values the Latin American heritage of Latinos, including various symbolic ties to Latin America. At the same time, this evolving audience profile asserts that most Latinos are not nostalgic about their Latin American cultural roots, or about returning "home" (with the exception of some Cuban American productions). Yet, a Latin American cultural identity is central to these bilingual Latino media. A common theme of these journalistic productions is a desire and/or a demand to have Latino ethnoracial identities within the larger U.S. society. These unresolvable tensions between elements of a U.S. and a Latin American identity are ambiguous and sometimes contradictory, and so not easily marketable.

Recently, media producers and marketers have begun to re-create the characteristics of the bilingual Hispanic audience as positive, potentially lucrative assets—as the future of the Hispanic media market. The *Tejano* (Texan) radio format, and youth-oriented Spanish language radio generally, broadcast mostly Spanish language contemporary music, prominently including rock *en Español.* The deejays routinely speak in Spanish and English (and Spanglish), and many of the local advertisements cross language lines, sometimes within the same phrase. For example, Levi's, the blue jean manufacturer, produced advertising with bilingual narration that ran mostly on Spanish language television stations in Houston and San Antonio.

A *Hispanic* cover story headlined "The Future of Spanish Language TV (in English)," profiles the flashiest of these bilingual efforts, a production company named Must Sí TV. Since 1997, it has aired two weekly 30-minute programs on *Galavisión,* a cable television network owned by *Univisión. Café Olé with Gisele Fernandez,* an interview program, and *Funny Is Funny,* a stand-up comedy showcase, are predominantly English language programs with an occasional Spanish phrase tossed in. Fernandez, a veteran English language journalist, told an interviewer, "My Spanish isn't as good as it could be, but it doesn't diminish the fact that I am Latina" (Doss, 1997, p. F1).

Jeff Valdez, the creator and producer of *Sí TV,* said he wants to provide entertainment programming to young Latinos who rarely, if ever, watch Spanish language television, those "who were raised on the Brady Bunch, not *Sábado Gigante.*" *Univisión* CEO Henry Cisneros said this programming is "an experiment," and is pleased with early ratings (Esparza, 1998; Zate, 1998a, 1998b, 1998c). In 1998, *Telemundo* also launched a mostly English language (with occasional Spanish and Spanglish phrases) talk show, hosted by actress Maria Conchita Alonso. Other English language and bilingual Hispanic media producers and marketers are exultant that the preeminent Spanish language Hispanic media companies have introduced the English language into their schedules. "It validates what we've been saying for years," chortled one.

BILINGUAL LATINO JOURNALISM

VISTA

VISTA (see Figure 7.1), "the magazine for all Hispanics," a monthly newspaper insert, is the most successful of bilingual Hispanic media, with a circulation of 1.2 million (according to a 1998 ABC audit). Founded in 1985, it is distributed nationally in 29 mostly English language newspapers concentrated in southwestern urban areas, as well as in New York, Chicago, and Miami. *VISTA,* currently owned by Hispanic Publications, Inc. (publisher of the English language magazine *Hispanic*), targets U.S.-born and -educated Hispanics. *VISTA* began as an English language magazine, and today remains largely English lan-

Figure 7.1. *VISTA* Cover

guage, with two Spanish language articles in each issue. (These are not translations of the magazine's English language articles but independent pieces.)

Like the newspaper insert *Parade* (with which it is often delivered, folded
into the middle of advertising-packed weekend newspapers), *VISTA*'s content is
upbeat. For example, a color-illustrated article profiles Latino Medal of Honor
winners, "the highest number of any ethnic group in the U.S." The 1998 editorial
calendar includes special reports on Hispanic elder care, as well as the World
Cup soccer championships. As *VISTA*'s mission statement proclaims, "Features
seek to inform and entertain, as well as to spotlight ordinary Hispanics who are
making extraordinary contributions to society."

VISTA has had a troubled existence. Key to its success—and failures—has
been its marketing and distribution formula. *VISTA* pays English language

newspapers to include the insert in issues delivered to retail outlets and homes in majority-Hispanic zip codes. From a marketing point of view, this is problematic: Most Hispanic zip codes are poorer areas, populated with consumers who are largely unattractive to advertisers. *VISTA* research shows that 49% of its readers have attended college, about half own their own homes, and more than 70% earn less than $50,000 a year (Roslow Research Group, 1998).

By instituting four regional issues (New York, Texas, Florida, and California), thereby further delineating the audience, *VISTA* has been able to allay some advertiser fears, and its operation is currently solvent. Its largest advertising category is cars (exclusively U.S. cars), followed by consumer products (soda, clothing, film, etc.) and recruitment ads by both government and corporate firms. *VISTA* describes its audience as the "most desirable Hispanic target audience" available at the lowest cost when compared to other Hispanic bilingual and English language publications.

Latina

Encouraged by language-use research discussed earlier, and particularly by the success of the special *People* editions on the death of Mexican American musician Selena (see Chapter 4), Christy Haubegger (a Mexican American Stanford Law School graduate) founded the magazine *bilingue Latina*. She comments,

> The stereotype is we don't read and we don't buy print. Our research says that just isn't true . . . I wanted to start a magazine for myself! Latinas live in a multilingual world . . . so much of our success is because we are bilingual . . . because our world is two worlds.

Latina is owned by Essence Publications (founded in 1969), publishers of the African American oriented magazines *Jet, Ebony,* and *Essence.* It claims that one of out ten African American women buys *Essence* each month. That extraordinarily high proportion of the target audience is unheard of in the general market and is, Haubegger says, a sign of the fierce loyalty only ethnic media can inspire. Paid circulation of *Latina* is 200,000, with a goal of 1 million by the turn of the century.

The Essence Publications sponsorship, key to *Latina*'s early success, is part of the parent company's long-term planning. "They [Essence executives] knew that soon there were going to be more of us [Latinos] than them [African Americans]," said a *Latina* audience researcher. Essence's backing (similar to Time Warner's launch of *People en Español*) is not solely a matter of deep corporate pockets providing millions for promotion and the cushioning of early losses.

Figure 7.2. *Latina* Cover

Equally important is the *Essence* distribution network made available to *Latina*. Prized newsstand, bookstore, and grocery store slots give new magazines critical exposure in the crowded, competitive magazine marketplace (see Figure 7.2).

Latina features articles about cosmetics and clothing and updated traditional recipes, like lower-fat enchiladas. In response to the scarcity of brown-eyed, olive-skinned models, *Latina* sponsored a contest for Latina models and signed the winner to a contract. Makeovers are a regular feature, as are celebrity profiles (e.g., Jennifer López, Salma Hayek, Gloria Estefan). Major advertisers—in both Spanish and English—have included Revlon, the Gap, and Ralph Lauren, as well as Kraft Foods, Procter & Gamble laundry detergents, and Chevrolet.

Latina's content reflects a broad conceptualization of its ethnoracially identified intended audience. *Latina* is 70% English language copy, 30% Spanish, usually printed in colored ink. "That's so it's easy to find," says Haubegger, who likes to think that each magazine is read by several generations of women, often in the same family. Articles about shaping eyebrows appear alongside features about parenting a bilingual child, the future of affirmative action, and the Latina glass ceiling. A feature called *"Triunfos*/Successes" profiles a new Chicana stand-up comedienne and the woman executive of a Puerto Rican nonprofit organization. *"Papi Chulo*/Our Finest Man," a photography-centered regular feature, shares space with pieces that run under the banner *"Lucha*/Coping" on topics ranging from stepfamilies to the challenges of producing a television arts magazine program. Other English language or bilingual magazines targeting Hispanic women, thus attempting to further segment the Hispanic audience by gender as well as by class, include *Qué Linda* (How Lovely), and *Latina Style*.

ENGLISH LANGUAGE LATINO JOURNALISM

Hispanic Business

Hispanic Business, published monthly since 1979, has adopted an assimilationist, class-based marketing discourse. In the words of *Hispanic Business* managing editor Hector Cantú, "We are going after the upscale reader. Most are fifth, sixth, and seventh generation. They are all middle or upper-middle class. [They are] assimilated in that they do business in English" (as quoted in Reilly, 1995, p. 60).

The editorial content of the magazine shuns the Spanish language, yet maintains a clear ethnic identification. It regularly features, for example, congratulatory profiles of successful Hispanic entrepreneurs, the annual top 500 Hispanic businesses ranked by their gross income, and "The Golden 50," the year's top Hispanic media advertisers. Specialized content and a Horatio-Alger-up-by-your-bootstraps tone—not the Spanish language—define *Hispanic Business* as an ethnoracial media.

The great majority (94.9%, according to a marketing survey) of *Hispanic Business*'s 225,000 readers do not pay for the magazine. Rather, in controlled circulation, readers receive complementary copies of the magazine because they are members of a Hispanic business group, such as the Hispanic Chamber of Commerce, or because they've requested it. Market research shows that less than a fifth of the magazine's readers earn less than $35,000 a year.

Most *Hispanic Business* readers, again according to commissioned market research, are "top management or are professionals." *Hispanic Business* has not inquired about the language usage of its readers. In addition to its publishing activities, *Hispanic Business* has sponsored an annual conference called *Se Habla Español* (Spanish spoken here) since the 1980s. In 1998, the Hispanic media trade show and exposition had a new name: Hispanic America 2000, One Market, Two Languages, *Un Mercado, Dos Idiomas. Hispanic Business* also sponsors HispanData, a resume service geared toward corporate recruitment of Hispanic managers and professionals.

Hispanic Business publishes three regional editions for the California, Florida, and Texas markets. The editorial copy is the same in each edition; the separate editions permit regional advertising. The magazine's largest advertisers include U.S. and Japanese automobile companies, business and financial services, and other private sector and government recruiters. Although shunning the Spanish language in its editorial copy, *Hispanic Business* accepts Spanish language and bilingual advertising.

Hispanic

Whereas *Hispanic Business* is targeting the business-oriented segment of the Hispanic elite, *Hispanic,* founded in 1987, is aiming for a broader slice of the Hispanic middle class. *Hispanic* was originally conceived as a *People* for Hispanics, but publisher Alfredo Estrada Jr. quickly discovered "there was no advertising base for that kind of a magazine." *Hispanic* shifted its focus to the business and career advertising categories, which are now its largest advertisers, followed by automobiles. Like *Hispanic Business* (its principal and perhaps only competition), *Hispanic,* with a circulation of 250,000, produces enthusiastic profiles of entrepreneurial Hispanics, but expands beyond the business sector to include Hispanic celebrities in many fields.

In 1996, Simmons Market Research (commissioned by *Hispanic*) reported that 83.7% of *Hispanic* readers had graduated from or attended college (according to the Census Bureau, 5.9% of Hispanics have college degrees, compared to 13.7% of non-Hispanics). The average household income of *Hispanic* readers is $69,520; the average household income for Hispanics nationally is about half that. According to publisher and editor Estrada (co-owner with his father of Hispanic Publications, Inc., which also publishes *VISTA*), the magazine's target audience is the roughly 15% of the Hispanic population that is "professional/managerial/white collar." Those 3 million Latinos, Estrada says, "include everyone from the CEO of a company to clerical workers.

"Some people view *Hispanic* magazine as very mainstream. Well, that's who we are. Our readership is very tied to corporate America, very tied to the American dream. It's very tied to success."

Two of the highest-profile activities of *Hispanic* are the annual ranking of the 100 best firms for Hispanics, and the *Adelante* (moving forward) awards presented to the 100 fastest-growing Hispanic-owned firms. Structurally, like *His-*

panic Business, Hispanic relies on advertising and controlled circulation, not paid circulation. Also like *Hispanic Business,* principal advertisers in *Hispanic* are corporate and government agency recruiters and automobiles.

Despite these similarities, *Hispanic*'s editorial voice distinguishes it from its principal rival. Unlike *Hispanic Business,* which rarely uses any Spanish words, *Hispanic* employs isolated Spanish language phrases as section headers. For example *"La Buena Vida"* (The Good Life) has restaurant, music, book, and film reviews of particular interest, and *"Avanzando"* (Getting Ahead) lists Hispanic career promotions. Each month several pages are taken up by a national Hispanic calendar of events, listing (by state) conferences, gallery openings, and other Hispanic cultural events. *Hispanic* produces profiles of educators and artists, along with articles about national and international politics, for example, federal and state immigration and affirmative action policies and the North American Free Trade Agreement (NAFTA).

In the last several years, *Hispanic*'s content has become more politically oriented and less focused on celebrity news. A 1998 cover story commemorating the 150th anniversary of the annexation of half of Mexico by the United States is a provocative historical essay. A series on Hispanics in higher education analyzes the post-affirmative-action challenges Hispanic students face. The regular *"BASTA!"* (Enough!) feature skewers stereotypical representations of Latinos. Overall, however, *Hispanic* is not controversial. Rather, it seeks to entertain middle-class Hispanics with information they are unlikely to find in general market magazines.

"Column of the Americas"

"Column of the Americas" (formerly known as "Latino Spectrum") is distributed by Universal Press Syndicate[2] to some 40 daily newspapers nationwide. These newspapers tend to be in Hispanic population centers and include the *Denver Post* and the *Los Angeles Times.* The individual newspapers can choose to run the column as it is written, weekly or less frequently. Written by Patrisia Gonzáles and Roberto Rodríguez, a university journalism professor and former *La Opinión* columnist, respectively, the column presents "news from a red/ brown perspective," Rodríguez said in a telephone interview.

A reading of a year's columns found that a clear ethnoracial framing is consistent throughout articles, which examine a range of topics from national electoral politics to global human rights. Most of the columns concern Latino politics. Some examples: A November 1997 column headlined (on its Internet publication) "Playing with Central American Lives" discusses the victims of the Communism Relief Act, a Congressional bill sponsored by Cuban American Congressional representatives that would have granted legal residency to Nicaraguans but not Guatemalans or El Salvadorans. Gonzáles and Rodríguez condemn the bill for prolonging the trauma of U.S.-financed Central American civil wars by rewarding only the anticommunist refugees the United States supports. Other columns defend MECHA, a Chicano student association; striking Latino farm workers; and the rights of Puerto Ricans to march in New York City in an annual parade in their honor. Some columns, although not losing their political edge, have a more spiritual tone. These include a moving tribute to the authors' immigrant mothers, and

> A New Year's prayer . . . prayers that were inspired while sitting . . . around a great fire, in which sage, tobacco and copal incense were offered with prayers for the new year . . . that the U.S. government (except for *la migra*) [the Immigration and Naturalization Service] discover the color brown. That goes for the Hollywood and entertainment industries with CNN taking the lead . . . that people learn to find happiness from within, rather than attaining it at the expense of others. And finally, that we quit blaming everything on that illegal alien El Niño. (January 3, 1998)

A shakeout in English language and bilingual Hispanic newsmaking is under way. For example, *Sí* (Yes), a *Vanity Fair* for Latinos, and *Frontera* (Border), which styled itself after *Harpers,* both folded within a year of their initial publication. *Moderna,* a sister publication of *Hispanic* and *VISTA,* was published for just 2 years. This is not unusual: It is a U.S. publishing industry truism that nine out of ten magazines don't survive their first 5 years. As Hispanic English language and bilingual publications fold, more are being attempted each year.

Politico

One of these Latino media startups is *Politico,* which in late 1998 was exclusively available on the Internet. Following the trail first blazed by *Hispanic Link* in 1982, *Politico* (Political), "the source for Latino political news," is a newsletter (only its name is in Spanish). Like *Hispanic Link,* which is widely distributed in Latino organizations (predominantly through photocopies), a large portion of *Politico*'s distribution is probably unpaid. *Politico* is distributed on the Internet, through e-mail subscriptions, and through Latino listservs. Editor James García[3] said in an interview that *Politico*'s readers are mostly Hispanic civic leaders active in their local Hispanic Chambers of Commerce, as well as in state capitals, Congress, and Hispanic lobbying groups.[4]

Weekly, *Politico* covers the broad landscape of Latino politics, offering news briefs concerning judicial rulings and electoral politics as well as summaries of Latin American political developments (provided by LATNN, the Latino Online News Network). *Politico* also features interviews, including, for instance, one with Newt Gingrich on the role of Latinos in the Republican party and the 1998 and 2000 elections. In addition, *Politico* publishes a national political Hispanic calendar.

What distinguishes *Politico* from most of the Latino newsmaking discussed in this book is its critical tone—critical of Hispanic organizations, as well as those that would deny Latinos political equity. Editor García said in a telephone interview that he is trying to offer something other than what he calls the "boosterism" of much of Latino-oriented journalism, adding that he thinks it is "hypocritical" to maintain that journalists don't have opinions.

Some examples: *Politico* took the National Association of Hispanic Publications (NAHP) to task for accepting funding from tobacco companies that encourage smoking by Hispanic youth. Following up on a story originally published in *Hispanic Business,* García condemned Jerold Perenchio's $300,000 contribution to California governor Pete Wilson's immigrant-bashing reelection campaign. Perenchio is the principal owner of *Univisión,* an enterprise dependent on Latino immigrant viewers. *Politico* declined to join the Hispanic voices lamenting the indictment of former San Antonio mayor and presidential cabinet secretary, currently *Univisión* CEO Henry Cisneros. Instead, *Politico* declared that Cisneros was a victim of his own arrogance.

All the Latino-oriented media discussed in this book, as well as more than 100 other Latino-oriented media firms—from weekly newspapers to radio programs—have Web sites featuring selected articles, and for broadcast media, transcriptions of interviews and stories.[5] Additionally, many sponsor chat rooms and/or listservs or newsgroups for their subscribers. Many of the larger non-media listservs, such as LaRED (The Network):

```
http://www.lared.es
```

and LaRED-L@Listserv.techrscs.panam.edu, carry news articles of particular Latino interest, as well as job postings and announcements of community events. Beyond a narrowly conceived journalistic or informational function, the Internet is a proving to be a site for the construction of panethnic, transnational Latino virtual communities.

For example, Latino Cyberraza from Ego-Web (`http://edb518ea.edb.utexas.edu/html/latinos.html`) is composed of hundreds of hypertext links to other Latino Web sites. Similarly, Electric Mercado (`http://www.mercado.com`) offers community newsletters and sections on Latino art and food as well as online shopping for Latin American products. Other Latino listservs, in Spanish or English or bilingually, facilitate discussions on such diverse topics as NAFTA, Chicano literature, and Caribbean folklore. Mundo Latino (`http://www.mundolatino.org`) is a Web site for Latinos who want to meet other Latinos and communicate with them in Spanish. Along the same lines, there are Web sites for Mexicans who want to meet other Mexicans online, Peruvians who would like to meet other Peruvians, and so on. Some of Latino communication on the Web, whether originating in the United States or Latin America, is conducted in its own language, what Rivas (1996) has dubbed *CyberSpanglish*.[6] Some examples:

English	CyberSpanglish	Spanish
apply	aplicar	solicitar
back up	hacer un backup, backupear	hacer un archivo de reserva
chat	chatear	conversar

The commonalities that unite Latino virtual communities are not very different from the social glue that binds other Latino media audiences: topics of particular, specialized interest; language; and a consciousness of a shared ethnoracial heritage.

NOTES

1. See the discussion of the born-again Hispanic audience in Chapter 4.
2. Universal Press Syndicate also distributes a column by Raul Yzaguirre, the president of the National Council of La Raza, a Washington, D.C., based Latino lobbying group.
3. García, a former Latin America reporter for Cox newspapers and the *Austin America Statesman,* is currently the editor of San Antonio's weekly alternative newspaper *The Current.*
4. In late 1998, García was in negotiations with investors interested in possible print publication of *Politico.*
5. This section draws on Rivas (1996).
6. A 500-entry CyberSpanglish dictionary is available at http://www.actlab.utexas.edu/seagull/spanglist.html

8

The Future of Latino Media
Suggestions for Further Research

The future of Latino media, like that of all media, turns on the media's ability to define and sell, and to attract and hold an audience. These complicated institutional processes are further muddied by the cultural, social, and political dynamics that shape media audiences. In the case of the Hispanic audience, Latino newsmaking and Hispanic media generally will be, as in the past, largely determined by political and cultural trends, primarily Latin American immigration to the United States and U.S. Latino adaptation and settlement patterns.

It is clear at this writing that despite stepped-up efforts by the U.S. federal government to curb immigration from south of the border, Latin American immigration has been only rerouted, not reduced. Entry points have shifted eastward away from the militarized Tijuana-San Diego border, but immigration has not significantly decreased. Indeed, the "structural embeddedness," the dependence of the United States on illegal Mexican immigrant labor, has been strengthened in the 1990s (Cornelius, 1998a, 1988b). Thus, the recent immigrant, monolingual Spanish speaking audience seems likely to be continually renewed.

Will continued Latin American immigration to the United States be sufficient to sustain Spanish language newspapers, magazines, and radio and television networks? Or will only firms with significant, complementary investment in Latin American, panhemispheric audiences, for example, *Editorial América, Univisión,* and CBS-*Telenoticias,* continue to thrive?

At the same time immigration from Latin America continues to affect the U.S. political cultural and economic landscape, the postwar trend for Latin American immigrants to put down roots and settle in the United States is continuing. Studies show that the children of recent immigrants, U.S. citizens by birth, are integrating into U.S. communities. The overwhelming majority are learning English; in what one scholar has called a "post Proposition 187 backlash," these young Latinos have a heightened sense of their Latino ethnoracial identity (Rumbaut, 1997).

How will consciousness of Latino ethnoracial identity—and increasing bilingual, as well as exclusive English language use, by Latinos—be reflected in Latino media? In other words, how will Latino-oriented media firms, as well as general market media, respond to the growth of the Latino population, both as permanent communities within the United States and as communities on society's fringes?

Insight can be gained from a consideration of African American communities and African American oriented journalism. Like African American news media, which have a continuous centuries-old tradition, Latino-oriented journalism will exist as long as Latinos are outside the center of U.S. society. As Berta Castañer, news director of the Chicago *Univisión* affiliate stated, "We serve the needs nobody else will, because they don't have to. It's as simple as that. We give them [the audience] information they can't get anywhere else." Whether Spanish or English language or both, Latino newsmaking is likely to endure as long as Latino communities have identifiable needs and interests not being served by other media. *La Opinión* marketing director Manny González puts it this way: "As long as civil rights and politics take center stage in our community, there will be a need for Hispanic media."

Cultural and political trends are but the broad framing of the future of Latino journalism. The perception of the media market and the audiencemaking Hispanic cultural industries are also critical. The entry (and expansion) of such major communication firms as Sony, CBS, Time Warner, Knight Ridder, and Times Mirror, as well as the continued presence of Latin American media companies in the Hispanic market, is a sign of confidence in its future.

The Hispanic audience, the bedrock of Latino journalism, has a niche in the U.S. media market as well as in the panhemispheric Latin American media market. Its central attribute, a conflation of Hispanic racialization and Spanish language use, has made the commercial and cultural construction called the "Hispanic audience" distinct. Being ethnoracially distinct, it is efficiently targetable. Being poor, it is twice marginalized.

For Latino newsmaking to survive, its audience profile needs to remain different, apart from the general market. That, in turn, ensures that Latino media will not become just another media, as many of its proponents would like. The central challenge of Latino media is likely to continue: to preserve a Latino ethnoracial identity and worldview, while at the same time embracing the defining values of the majority society and its media market.

References

Acuña, R. (1988). *Occupied America: A history of Chicanos* (3rd ed.). New York: Harper Collins.

Aguilar, L. (1997, December). Time's Latino section opposed. *Hispanic, 10*(11), 10-12.

Anderson, B. (1986). *Imagined communities: Reflections on the origin and spread of nationalism.* London: Verso Editions and NLB.

Ang, I. (1991). *Desperately seeking the audience.* London: Routledge.

Astroff, R. J. (1988). Spanish gold: Stereotypes, ideology, and the construction of a U.S. Latino market. *Howard Journal of Communication, 1,*(4), 155-173.

Barbero, J. M. (1987). *Communication, culture, and hegemony: From the media to mediations.* Thousand Oaks, CA: Sage.

Barnes, B. E., & Thomson, L. M. (1994). Power to the people (meter): Audience measurement technology and media specialization. In J. S. Ettema & D. C. Whitney (Eds.), *Audiencemaking: How the media create the audience* (pp. 75-95). Thousand Oaks, CA: Sage.

Barnouw, E. (1963). *A history of broadcasting in the United States, Volume 1, A Tower of Babel, to 1933.* New York: Oxford University Press.

Bauman, R. (1993). Introduction. In R. Bauman (Ed.), *Folklore and culture on the Texas-Mexican border* (pp. ix-xxiii). Austin: University of Texas Press.

Baxter, K. (1997a, August 21). LA's Spanish media face a new Latino reality. *Los Angeles Times,* p. F51.

Baxter, K. (1997b, December 11). Around the dial: An experiment in unity; Backers of *Radio Unica* say the U.S. market is ready for a 24-hour Spanish-language network. *Los Angeles Times,* p. F22.

Baxter, K. (1998, September 21). Spanish language networks seek wider niche. *Los Angeles Times,* p. F5.

Beale, L. (1983, June 26). SIN network: News from a Latino perspective. *Los Angeles Times,* pp. C85-C86.

Bean, F. D., Edmonston, B., & Passel, J. S. (Eds.). (1990). *Undocumented migration to the United States: IRCA and the experience of the 1980's.* Santa Monica, CA, and Washington, DC: RAND and Urban Institute.

Bean, F. D., & Tienda, M. (1987). *The Hispanic population of the United States.* New York: Russell Sage.

Bechloss, S. (1990, July 15). The missing pot of gold. *Channels, 10*(10), 30-36.

Benson, J. (1996, April 17). KLVE, a.m. DJ Barret top Arbitron Radio ratings. *Daily Variety,* p. 2.

Berg, C. R. (1990). Stereotyping in films in general and of the Hispanic in particular. *Howard Journal of Communication, 2,*(3), 286-300.

Blauner, R. (1972). *Racial oppression in America.* New York: Harper & Row.

Blumenthal, R. G. (1990, February 2). *Univisión* fails to pay interest to banks, holders. *Wall Street Journal,* p. B17.

Brodesser, C. (1997, July 21). Miami TV stations: Nielsen under fire on Hispanic sample. *Media Week, 7,* 29.

Bureau of the Census. (1997). *Statistical abstract of the United States: 1997* (117th ed.). Washington, DC: Author.

Bureau of Labor Statistics. (1995). *Supplement to the current population survey.* Washington, DC: Government Printing Office.

Bussey, J., & Arrarte, A. M. (1993, January 25). Cadena de TV en español compiten con tácticas divergentes. *El Nuevo Herald,* pp. 3-4B.

Carey, J. W. (1986). The dark continent of American journalism. In R. K. Manoff & M. Schudson (Eds.), *Reading the news.* New York: Pantheon.

Carey, J. W. (1992). *Communication as culture: Essays on media and society.* New York: Unwin Hyman.

Carnevale, M. L. (1992, October 1). Sale of U.S. television stations to Azcárraga group is cleared by FCC. *Wall Street Journal,* pp. B8, B11.

Census Bureau. (1997). *Historical income tables—Families, race and Hispanic origin of householder—Families by median and mean income, 1967-1997.* http://www/census.gov/hhes/income/histinc/f05.html

Chácon, R. D. (1997). The Chicano immigrant press in Los Angeles: The case of "El Heraldo de México": 1916-1920. *Journalism History, 4*(2), 48-50, 63.

Chavira, R. (1977). A case study: Reporting of Mexican emigration and deportation. *Journalism History, 4*(2), 59-61.

Cornelius, W. A. (1992). From sojourners to settlers: The changing profile of Mexican immigration to the United States. In J. A. Bustamante, C. W. Reynolds, & R. A. Hinojosa Ojeda (Eds.), *U.S.-Mexico relations: Labor market interdependence.* Stanford, CA: Stanford University Press.

Cornelius, W. A. (1995). Educating California's immigrant children: Introduction and overview. In R. Rumbaut & W. A. Cornelius (Eds.), *California's immigrant children: Theory, research and implications for educational policy* (pp. 1-16). San Diego: University of California, Center for U.S.-Mexican Studies.

Cornelius, W. A (1998a). Appearance and realities: Controlling illegal immigration in the United States. In M. Weiner & T. Hanami (Eds.), *Temporary workers or future citizens? Japanese and U.S. migration policies* (pp. 384-427). New York: New York University Press.

Cornelius, W. A. (1998b). The structural embeddedness of demand for Mexican immigrant labor: New evidence from California. In M. M. Suárez-Orozco (Ed.), *Crossings: Mexican immigration and interdisciplinary perspectives* (pp. 115-144). Cambridge, MA: Harvard University Press.

Cornell, S. E. (1988). *The return of the native: American Indian political resurgence.* New York: Oxford University Press.

Cortes, C. E. (1987). The Mexican-American press. In S. Miller (Ed.), *The ethnic press in the United States: A historical analysis and handbook.* New York: Greenwood.

Cropper, C. M. (1998, July 10). Spanish speaking consumers are the object of a growing number of marketer's desires. *New York Times,* p. C5.

Davies, J. (1997, August 21). LA stations wary of plan to blend in Hispanic viewership figures. *Hollywood Reporter,* p. 3.

de la Garza, R. (1992). *Latino voices: Mexican, Puerto Rican and Cuban perspectives on American politics.* Hartford, CT: Westview.

de la Garza, R., et al. (1996). *1996 national Latino voter survey* [mimeo]. Austin: University of Texas at Austin, Government Department.

del Olmo, F. (1986, January 23). Spanish language TV needs Latino American's input. *Los Angeles Times,* Part 2, p. 5.

Department of Justice. (1995). *1995 Statistical Yearbook of the Immigration and Nationalization Service.* Washington, DC: Author.

de Uriarte, M. (1980, December 14). Battle for the ear of the Latino. *Los Angeles Times,* p. F5.

Didion, J. (1987). *Miami.* New York: Pocket Books.

DeSipio, L. (1998). *Talking back to television: Latinos discuss how television portrays them and the quality of programming options.* Claremont, CA: Tomás Rivera Policy Institute.

Doss, Y. C. (1997, November 8). A Spanish language network tries bilingualism. *Los Angeles Times,* pp. F1, F8.

Douglas, N. (1996). Purchasing power at $223 billion. *Hispanic, 9*(11), 48.

DRI/McGraw-Hill. (1993). The use of the Spanish language in the United States: Executive summary. Lexington, MA: Author.

DRI/McGraw-Hill. (1994). *Hispanic language study.* New York: Author.

Edwards, J. (1975). *Language, society and identity.* London: Basil Blackwell in association with Andre Deutsch.

Entman, R. M. (1990). Modern racism and the images of blacks in local television news. *Critical Studies in Mass Communication, 7,* 332-345.

Ericksen, C. (1981). Hispanic Americans and the press. *Journal of Intergroup Relations, 9*(1), 3-16.

Esparza, E. (1998, May). The future of Spanish language TV (in English): Must see TV. *Hispanic, 11*(6), 20, 28.

Espinosa, P. (Producer). (1982). *Break of dawn: Ballad of an unsung hero.* New York: Public Broadcasting Service.

Espiritu, Y. L. (1992). *Asian-American panethnicity: Bridging institutions and identities.* Philadelphia: Temple University Press.

Ettema, J. S., & Whitney, D. C. (1994). *Audiencemaking: How the media create the audience.* Thousand Oaks, CA: Sage.

Fishman, J. (1972). *Language in sociocultural change.* Palo Alto, CA: Stanford University Press.

Fishman, J. (1989). *Language and ethnicity in minority sociolinguistic perspective.* Clarendon, UK: Multilingual Matters Ltd.

Flores-Hughes, G. (1996, September). Why the term "Hispanic"? *Hispanic, 9*(6), 64.

Fowler, G., & Crawford, B. (1987). *Border radio: Quacks, yodelers, pitchmen, psychics, and other amazing broadcasters of the American airwaves.* Austin: Texas Monthly Press.

Freeman, M. (1998). *1998 U.S. Hispanic market study.* Miami: PM Communications Inc.

Fuchs, L. H. (1990). *The American kaleidoscope: Race, ethnicity, and the civic culture.* Hanover, CT: Wesleyan University Press.

Gandy, O. H. (1998). *Communication and race: A structural perspective.* London and New York: Arnold and Oxford University Press.

Gans, H. J. (1979). *Deciding what's news: A study of CBS Evening News, NBC Nightly News, Newsweek and Time.* New York: Vintage.

García Canclini, N. (1995). *Hybrid cultures: Strategies for entering and leaving modernity* (C. L. Chiappari & S. L. López, Translators). Minneapolis: University of Minnesota Press.

García, M. T. (1989). *Mexican-Americans: Leadership, ideology and identity, 1930-1960.* New Haven, CT: Yale University Press.

García, M. T. (1995). *Rubén Salazar: Border correspondent.* Berkeley: University of California Press.

Gerbner, G. (1993). *Women and minorities on television: A study in casting and fate.* Philadelphia: University of Pennsylvania, Annenberg School of Communication.

Gitlin, T. (1983). *Inside prime time.* New York: Pantheon.

Goldberg, C. (1997, January 30). Hispanic households struggle as poorest of the poor in U.S. *New York Times,* p. 1, A12.

Gonzáles, A. (1998, Spring). Immigrants, language acquisition and economic gain. *The Arizona Report,* pp. 4-5.

Gray, H. (1989). Television, black Americans, and the American dream. *Critical Studies in Mass Communication, 6,* 376-386.

Gray, H. (1995). *Watching race: Television and the struggle for blackness.* Minneapolis: University of Minnesota Press.

Grebler, L., Moore, J. W., & Guzman, R. (1970). *The Mexican-American people: The nation's second largest minority.* New York: Free Press.

Greenberg, B., & Brand, J. E. (1994). Minorities and the mass media: 1970's to 1990's. In O. Bryan & D. Zillmann (Eds.), *Media effects: Advances in theory and research.* Hillsdale, NJ: Lawrence Erlbaum.

Griswold del Castillo, R. (1977). The Mexican revolution and the Spanish language press in the badlands. *Journalism History, 4*(2), 42-48.

Gutiérrez, F. (1977). Spanish language media in America: Background, resources, history. *Journalism History, 4*(2), 34-42.

Gutiérrez, F., & Schement, J. R. (1979). *Spanish language radio in the southwestern United States.* Austin: University of Texas at Austin, Center for Mexican-American Studies.

Gutiérrez F., & Schement, J. R. (1984). Spanish International Network: The flow of television from Mexico to the United States. *Communication Research, 11*(2), 241-258.

Hall, S. (1979). Culture, the media and the "ideological effect." In J. Curran, M. Gurevitch, & J. Woolacott (Eds.), *Mass communication and society* (pp. 315-345). Beverly Hills, CA: Sage.

Hall, S. (1990). Cultural identity and diaspora. In R. Jonathan (Ed.), *Identity, community, culture, difference* (pp. 222-237). London: Lawrence & Wishart.

Hall, S. (1992). The new ethnicities. In J. Donald & S. Nattansi (Eds.), *"Race," culture and difference* (pp. 252-259). London: Sage in association with The Open University.

Hall, S. (1993). Culture, community, nation. *Cultural Studies, 7,* 349-374.

Hallin, D. C. (1985). The American news media: A critical theory perspective. In J. M. Forrester (Ed.), *Critical theory and public life.* Boston: MIT Press.

Hallin, D. C. (1986). We keep America on top of the world. In T. Gitlin (Ed.), *Watching television.* New York: Pantheon.

Hallin, D. C., & Mancini, P. (1984). Speaking of the president: Political structure and representational form in U.S. and Italian television news. *Theory and Society, 13,* 829-850.

Handlin, O. (1979). *Boston's immigrants, 1790-1880: A study in acculturation.* Cambridge, MA: Belknap. (Original work published 1941)

Hart-González, L. (1985). Pan Hispanism and sub-community in Washington, DC. In L. E. Olivares et al. (Eds.), *Spanish language use and public life in the United States* (pp. 73-89). New York: Mouton.

Harvey, D. (1989). *The condition of postmodernity: An enquiry into the origins of cultural change.* Oxford: Basil Blackwell.

Hayes, J. (1993). Early Mexican radio broadcasting: Media imperialism, state paternalism or Mexican nationalism? *Studies in Latin American Popular Culture, 12,* 31-55.

Hersch, S. (1997). *The dark side of Camelot.* Boston: Little, Brown.

Higham, J. (1985). *Strangers in the land: Patterns of American nativism, 1860-1925.* New Brunswick, NJ: Rutgers University Press. (Original work published 1955)

Hispanic market report. (1997). *Hispanic Business, 19*(12).

Hobsbawn, E. (1983). Introduction: Inventing traditions. In E. Hobsbawn & T. Ranger (Eds.), *The invention of tradition.* Cambridge: Cambridge University Press.

Horwitz, R. (1989). *The irony of deregulatory reform: The deregulation of American telecommunications.* New York: Oxford University Press.

Jolson-Colburn, J. (1996, April 17). KLVE-FM, Baretto stay on top. *The Hollywood Reporter,* p. 1.

Kanellos, N. (Ed.). (1993). *The Hispanic almanac: A reference work on Hispanics in the United States.* Detroit: Gates Research, Inc.

Keever, B. A. D., Martindale, C., & Weston, M. A. (1997). *U.S. news coverage of racial minorities: A sourcebook, 1934-1996.* Westport, CT: Greenwood.

Kessler, L. (1984). *The dissident press: Alternative journalism in American history.* Beverly Hills, CA: Sage.

Landry, R. J. (1946). *This fascinating radio business.* Indianapolis and New York: Bobbs-Merrill.

La Prensa. (1989). [Special issue]. *America's Review, 17,*(3-4).

Lichter, S. R., & Lichter, L. (1988). *Television's impact on ethnic and racial images: A study of Howard Beach adolescents.* New York: American Jewish Committee.

Lichter, S. R., Lichter, L., & Rothman, S. (1991). *Watching America.* New York: Prentice Hall.

Lippman, J., & Darling, J. (1993, May 20). US, Mexican firms team up to offer pay TV in Latin America. *Los Angeles Times,* p. D1.

Lipsitz, G. (1998). *The possessive investment in whiteness: How white people profit from identity politics.* Philadelphia: Temple University Press.

Lopes, H. (1993, February). Bad vibes but good business? Despite strong Nielsen numbers, new bosses at *Univisión* trim work force. *Hispanic Business,* pp. 30-32, 34, 36.

López, B. (1997). Balancing act: Surviving as a television reporter in Mexico. In W. A. Orme (Ed.), *A culture of collusion: An inside look at the Mexican press* (pp. 89-97). Miami, FL: University of Miami, North-South Center Press.

López, D., & Espiritu, Y. L. (1990). Panethnicity in the United States: A theoretical framework. *Ethnic and Racial Studies, 3*(2), 198-224.

MacLean, E. (1998). *Vanidades and the construction of a pan-American Hispanic female audience.* Unpublished master's thesis, University of Texas, Austin.

Martindale, C. (1995, August). *Only in glimpses: Portrayal of America's largest minority groups in the New York Times, 1934-1994.* Paper presented at the Association for Education in Journalism and Mass Communication, Washington, DC.

McChesney, R. W. (1994). *Telecommunications, mass media and democracy: The battle for control for the control of U.S. broadcasting, 1928-1935.* New York: Oxford University Press.

McManus, J. H. (1994). *Market driven journalism: Let the citizen beware.* Thousand Oaks, CA: Sage.

McWilliams, C. (1968). *North from Mexico: The Spanish speaking people of the United States.* New York: Greenwood.

Medeiros, F. (1980). *La Opinión:* A Mexican exile newspaper: A content analysis of its first years, 1926-1929. *Aztlan, 5*(1), 66-80.

Meehan, E. R. (1984). Ratings and the institutional approach: A third answer to the commodity question. *Critical Studies in Mass Communication, 1,* 216-225.

Meluza, L. (1986, December 14). Borrador. *El Miami Herald,* p. 2.

Melville, M. B. (1988). Hispanics: Race, class or ethnicity? *Journal of Ethnic Studies, 16,* 67-83.

Michaelson, J. (1996, April 17). *House party* gives KKBT-FM a lift in the Arbitron ratings. *Los Angeles Times,* pp. F1, F8.

Miller, S. (Ed.). (1987). *The ethnic press in the United States: A historical analysis and handbook.* New York: Greenwood.

Mosco, V. (1996). *The political economy of communication: Rethinking and renewal.* Thousand Oaks, CA: Sage.

Molina, G. G. (1992). *Televisa: An organizational analysis.* Unpublished doctoral dissertation, University of Texas, Austin.

Moore, J., & Pachón, H. (1985). *Hispanics in the United States.* Englewood Cliffs, NJ: Prentice-Hall.

Morales, E. (1996, July 30). Brownout: Latinos are America's fastest growing minority, but not in the newsroom. *Villiage Voice,* pp. 25-29.

Morley, D., & Robbins, K. (1995). *Spaces of identity: Global media, electronic landscapes and cultural boundaries.* London: Routledge.

Moss, A. M. (1996). *Audience identity construction within four Latino-oriented community newspapers.* Unpublished master's thesis, University of Texas, Austin.

Mydans, S. (1989, August 27). TV unites and divides Hispanic groups. *New York Times,* p. 4.

National Council of La Raza. (1998, August). *News brownout.* Report presented at the Hispanic Association of Journalists meetings, Miami, Florida.

Navarrete, L., & Kamasaki, C. (1994). *Out of the picture, Hispanics in the media: State of Hispanic America, 1994.* Washington, DC: National Council of *La Raza.*

Navarro, M. (1997a, April 6). Inside Miami's Little Havana, a quiet change of accents. *New York Times,* pp. A1, A12.

Navarro, M. (1997b, November 1). Miami election for mayor rouses sour mood in voters. *New York Times,* p. A17.

Nelson, C., & Tienda, M. (1985). The structuring of Hispanic ethnicity: Historical and contemporary perspectives. *Ethnic and Racial Studies, 8*(1), 49-74.

New America. [Videotape]. (1996). Miami, FL: *Univisión.*

Nielsen Media Research. (1998). *National Hispanic Television Index.* New York: Author.

Noriega, A., & Leach, F. (1979). *Broadcasting in Mexico.* London: Routledge Kegan Paul in association with International Institute of Communications.

Novoa, B. (Ed.). (1989). La Prensa and the Chicano community. *America's Review, 17*(3-4), 121-184.

Nuiry, O. E. (1996, December). Magazine mania. *Hispanic,* pp.53-57.

Oboler, S. (1995). *Ethnic labels, Latino lives: Identity and the politics of (re)presentation in the United States.* Minneapolis: University of Minnesota Press.

Omi, M., & Winant, H. (1986). *Racial formation in the United States.* London: Routledge Kegan Paul.

Padilla, F. M. (1985). *Latino ethnic consciousness: The case of Mexican-Americans and Puerto Ricans in Chicago.* Notre Dame, IN: University of Notre Dame Press.

Paredes, A. (1958). *With his pistol in his hand: A border ballad and its hero.* Austin: University of Texas Press.

Parillo, V. (1979). *Rethinking today's minorities.* New York: Greenwood.

Park, R. (1922). *The immigrant press and its control.* New York: Harper.

Paulsen, M. (1998, September 25). *El Polvo:* Intruders in the dust. *Texas Observer,* pp. 10-16.

Pedro González. (1995, March 24). *New York Times,* p. C20.

Peterson, I. (1997, November 17). At Los Angeles Times, a debate on news-ads interaction. *New York Times,* pp. B1, B11.

Pollack, A. (1997, November 25). Entering U.S. broadcasting, Sony buys *Telemundo* stake. *New York Times,* p. C8.

Pollack, A. (1998, January 19). The fight for Hispanic viewers: *Univisión's* success story attracts new competition. *New York Times,* pp. C1, C6.

Porter, T. M. (1995). *Trust in numbers: The pursuit of objectivity in science and public life*. Princeton, NJ: Princeton University Press.

Portes, A., & Bach, R. (1985). *Latin journey: Cuban and Mexican immigrants in the United States*. Berkeley: University of California Press.

Portes, A., & Truelove, C. (1987). Making sense of diversity: Recent research on Hispanic minorities in the United States. *Annual Review of Sociology, 13*, 359-385.

Pozzeita, G. (Ed.). (1991). *American immigration and ethnicity: Immigrant institutions: The organization of immigrant life* (Vol. 5). New York: Garland.

Puig, C. (1992, August 10). Piden al Departamento de Justicia que no autorice la venta de *Univisión* a Azcárraga: Temor que lleve a Estados Unidos las prácticas de Televisa. *Proceso, 823,* pp. 20-22, 25.

Rasky, S. (1997). The media covers Los Angeles. *California Journal, 28*(7), 42-46.

Reilly, J. L. (1995). *Views of Mexico since NAFTA: Representations in national U.S. Hispanic publications*. Unpublished master's thesis, University of Texas, Austin.

Riding, A. (1984). *Distant neighbors: A portrait of the Mexicans*. New York: Knopf.

Rios-McMillan, V. (1989). La Prensa de San Antonio. *America's Review, 17*(3-4), 130-143.

Rivas, Y. (1996). *Emergence of Latino panethnic communities on the Internet: Expressions within a new medium*. Unpublished master's thesis, University of Texas, Austin.

Rodriguez, A. (1993). *Made in the USA: The constructions of the Noticiero Univisión*. Unpublished doctoral dissertation, University of California, San Diego.

Rodriguez, A. (1996). Objectivity and ethnicity in the production of the *Noticiero Univisión*. *Critical Studies in Mass Communication, 13*(1), 59-82.

Rodriguez, A. (1997). Commercial ethnicity: Language, class and race in the marketing of Hispanic audience. *Communication Reviews, 2*(3), 283-311.

Rodriguez, A. (1999). Creating an audience and remapping a nation: A brief history of U.S. Spanish language broadcasting, 1930-1980. *Quarterly Review of Film and Video, 16*(3-4).

Rodríguez, C. (1989). Puerto Ricans: The rainbow people. In V. Parillo (Ed.), *Puerto Ricans: Born in the USA* (pp. 87-118). New York: Unwin Hyman.

Rodríguez, C. (1991). Puerto Ricans: The rainbow people. V. Parillo (Ed.), *Rethinking today's minorities*. New York: Greenwood.

Rodríguez, C., & Cordero-Guzman, H. (1992). Placing race in context. *Ethnic and Racial Studies, 15,* 4.

Rodriguez, G. (1996, September 2). The browning of California: Proposition 187 backfires. *New Republic,* pp. 10, 18-19.

Romo, R. (1983). *East Los Angeles: History of the barrio*. Austin: University of Texas Press.

Roslow Research Group. (1998). *VISTA audience profile*. Miami: Author.

Rumbaut, R. (1991). The agony of exile: A study of the migration and adaptation of Indochinese refugee adults and children. In F. Ahearn & J. Athey (Eds.), *Refugee children: Theory, research and services*. Baltimore: Johns Hopkins University Press.

Rumbaut, R. (1997, June 18). *Passages to adulthood: The adaptation of children of immigrants in Southern California*. Report to the Russell Sage Foundation, New York.

Sánchez, G. J. (1993). *Becoming Mexican-American: Ethnicity, culture and identity in Chicano Los Angeles, 1900-1945.* New York: Oxford University Press.

Saragoza, A. (1987, October). Paper presented at the Department of Communication, University of California, San Diego.

Scarborough Research. (1995a). *The Los Angeles Hispanic Market.* New York: Author.

Scarborough Research. (1995b). *The Miami Hispanic Market.* New York: Author.

Schement, J. R., & Flores, R. (1977). The origins of Spanish language radio: The case of San Antonio, Texas. *Journalism History, 4*(2), 56-59.

Schement, J. R., & Singleton, R. A. (1981). The onus of minority ownership: FCC policy and the Spanish language radio. *Journal of Communication, 31*(2), 78-83.

Schiller, D. (1981). *Objectivity and the news: The public and the rise of commercial journalism.* Philadelphia: University of Pennsylvania Press.

Schlesinger, P. (1987). On national identity: Some conceptions and misconceptions criticized. *Social Science Information, 26*(2), 219-264.

Schlesinger, P. (1991). Media, political order, and national identity. *Media, Culture, and Society, 13,* 197-308.

Schudson, M. (1978). *Discovering the news: A social history of America's newspapers.* New York: Basic Books.

Schudson, M. (1982). The politics of narrative form: The emergence of news conventions in print and television. *Daedlus, 111,* 97-113.

Schudson, M. (1984). *Advertising, the uneasy persuasion: Its dubious impact on American society.* New York: Basic Books.

Schudson, M. (1991). National news culture and the rise of the informational citizen. In A. Wolfe (Ed.) *America at century's end.* Berkeley: University of California Press.

Schudson, M. (1995). *The power of news.* Cambridge, MA: Harvard University Press.

Shorris, E. (1992). *Latinos: A biography of a people.* New York: Norton.

Sigal, L. V. (1973). *Reporters and officials: The organization and politics of newsmaking.* Lexington, MA: D.C. Heath.

Simmons Hispanic Market Research. (1996). *Hispanic market research report.* New York: Author.

Simonson, R., & Walker, S. (1988). Documented/undocumented. In R. Simonson & S. Walker (Eds.), *Multi-cultural literacy: Opening the American mind* (p. 127). Saint Paul, MN: Graywolf.

SIN launched. (1981, September 21). *Television/Radio Age,* pp. 45-46.

Sinclair, J. (1991). Spanish language television in the United States: *Televisa* surrenders its domain. *Studies in Latin American Popular Culture, 9,* 42.

Sinclair, J. (1996). Culture and trade: Some theoretical and practical considerations. In E. G. McAnany & K. T. Wilkinson (Eds.), *Mass media and free trade* (pp. 30-62). Austin: University of Texas Press.

Sommers, L. K. (1991). Inventing Latinismo: The creation of "Hispanic" panethnicity in the United States. *Journal of American Folklore, 7,* 104-112.

Steingold, J. (1997, October 13). A growing clash of visions at the Los Angeles Times. *New York Times,* pp. B1, B8.

Streeter, T. (1987). The cable fable revisited: Discourse, policy, and the making of cable television. *Critical Studies in Mass Communication, 4,* 174-200.

Stuteville, J. R., & Roberts, M. D. (1975). *Marketing in a consumer oriented society.* Belmont, CA: Wadsworth.

Subervi Vélez, F. (1994). Mass communication and Hispanics. In N. Kanellos (Ed.), *Handbook of Hispanic cultures in the United States* (pp. 317-319). Houston, TX: Arte Publico.

Television and Radio Age. (1981). [Trade journal].

Tiegel, E. (1995, December 18). LA Spanish stations thrive: 14 radio, 4 TV outlets serve a diverse Hispanic audience. *Electronic Media,* p. 20D.

Torres, M. (1997, December 1). Autumn of the Cuban patriarchs. *The Nation,* p. 24.

Tuchman, G. (1972). Objectivity as a strategic ritual: An examination of newsmen's notions of objectivity. *Journal of Sociology, 77,* 4.

Tuchman, G. (1978). *Making news: A study in the construction of reality.* New York: Free Press.

Turner, R. (1997, October 20). Snap, crackle, pop: The LA Times gets a new start minus its editor. *Newsweek,* pp. 62-63.

Turow, J. (1997). *Breaking up America: Advertisers and the new media world.* Chicago: University of Chicago Press.

U.S. Bureau of the Census. (1995). *Hispanic Americans today.* Washington, DC: Department of Commerce.

U.S. Bureau of the Census. (1996). (1995). *Statistical abstracts of the United States.* Washington, DC: Department of Commerce.

Univisión seeing red ink. (1990, February, 19). *Broadcasting,* p. 62.

Urciuoli, B. (1996). *Exposing prejudice: Puerto Rican experiences of language, race and class.* Boulder, CO: Westview.

Valenzuela, N. A. (1985). *Organizational evolution of a Spanish language television network: An environmental approach.* Unpublished doctoral dissertation, Stanford University, Stanford, CA.

Valle, V. (1986, September 21). The SIN sale: Will it make any difference? *Los Angeles Times,* p. F22.

Valle, V. (1987). Latino groups hit FCC Hallmark ruling. *Los Angeles Times,* June 5, F2.

Warshauer, M. E. (1975). Foreign language broadcasting. In J. Fishman (Ed.), *Language loyalties* (pp. 81-101). Stanford, CA: Stanford University Press.

Weiner, T. (1998, February 22). CIA bares its bungling in report on Bay of Pigs invasion. *New York Times,* p. A6.

Weinstein, S. (1996, May 28). Arbitron poll to clarify who's listening. *Los Angeles Times,* p. F1, F9.

Whistler, K. (1998). *The national Hispanic media directory* (copyright WPR), as reprinted in *Hispanic Print: Abriendo Caminos to the Hispanic Market.* National Association of Hispanic Publishers.

Wilkinson, K. (1991). *The sale of Spanish International Communications Corporation: Milestone in the development of Spanish language television in the United States.* Unpublished master's thesis, University of California, Berkeley.

Wilkinson, K. (1995). *Where culture, language and communication converge: The Latin American cultural linguistic television market.* Unpublished doctoral dissertation, University of Texas, Austin.

Williams, R. (1980). Base and superstructure in Marxist cultural theory. In R. Williams (Ed.), *Problems in materialism and culture* (pp. 31-49). London: Verso.

Williams, R. (1983). *Keywords: A vocabulary of culture and society.* New York: Oxford University Press.

Wilson, C. W., & Gutiérrez, F. (1995). *Race, multiculturalism, and the media: From mass to class communication* (2nd ed.). Thousand Oaks, CA: Sage.

Winant, H. (1994). *Racial conditions: Politics, theory, comparisons.* Minneapolis: University of Minnesota Press.

Woolard, K. A. (1985). Language variation and cultural hegemony: Toward an integration of sociolinguistic and social theory. *American Ethnologist, 12*(4), 738-748.

Yankelovich, Skelly, and White. (1981). *Spanish USA.* New York: Author.

Ynclan, N. (1984, January/February). Thunder on the right in Miami. *Columbia Journalism Review,* pp. 9-11.

Zate, M. (1998a, March). Launch of a new TV era? *Hispanic Business,* p. 14.

Zate, M. (1998b, May). The big picture: Original programming with shows unique to the cultural experiences of Hispanics is coming to a Spanish language television near you. *Hispanic Business,* pp. 26, 28, 30.

Zate, M. (1998c). TV, magazines, and newspapers: Beyond Español, New York: *News America News Service.*

Zubrycki, J. (1992). The role of the foreign language press in migrant integration. In J. Folkerts (Ed.), *Media voices: A historical perspective: An anthology.* New York: Macmillan.

Index

voter registration, 22, 118
Electric Mercado, 143
English language, use by Latinos, 56, 132, 133, 146
English language media:
   magazines, 133, 139-141, 142
   See also General market media
El Espectador, 19-21
Essence magazine, 137
Essence Publications, 137-138
Estrada, Alfredo, Jr., 140
Ethnicity, 6
European immigrants, 34-35

Falcón, Alina, 87-88
FCC. *See* Federal Communications Commission
Federal Communications Commission (FCC), 62, 63, 65, 86
Fernandez, Gisele, 135
Florida:
   Cuban immigrants, 4, 38, 40, 108, 124
   radio stations, 58
   See also Miami
Foucé, Frank, Jr., 62
Frontera magazine, 142
El Fronterizo, 15

Galavisión, 135
Gans, H. J., 85
García, James, 142, 143
García, Mario, 20
García, Robert, 42
General market media:
   advertising rates, 54
   audience for television news, 94-95
   exclusion of Latinos, 2, 95, 96
   international news, 99, 101, 110
   Latino journalists employed by, 23, 110, 111, 127
   Latino news, 2, 95, 111-112, 127
   portrayal of Latinos, 2, 41
   service-oriented journalism, 108
   See also Newspapers, English language; Television news, English language
Gingrich, Newt, 143
Gitlin, T., 68-69
Godoy, Gustavo, 80, 86
Gómez-Peña, Guillermo, 26
Gonzáles, Patrisia, 141-142

Gonzalez, Henry B., 19
González, Manny, 111, 146
González, Pedro, 29
Goya Foods, 82
Grimes, Bill, 52
Guatemala, immigrants from, 109
Gutiérrez, Barbara, 121, 123, 124
Gutiérrez, Luis, 99
Guzmán, Armando, 91, 104

Hallin, D. C., 88
Hallmark, Inc., 52, 61, 63, 64
Haubegger, Christy, 137
El Heraldo de Brownsville, 24
El Heraldo de México, 16
Hispanic:
   as ethnoracial category, 27
   as racial category, 6, 49-50
   rejection of term, 43
   use of term, 39, 41, 42
Hispanic audience:
   American patriotism of, 54-55
   bilingual, 56, 131-134, 137, 146
   characteristics, 47
   class differences, 49, 58-59
   creation of, 38-40, 43-44, 47, 48, 54-55, 66-67
   definition, 5, 26
   discovery of, 41
   economic importance, 29, 51
   English language use, 56, 132, 133, 146
   ethnic identity, 67, 146
   for local television news, 107-108
   for television news, 56, 69-70, 78, 84, 94-95, 127-128
   future of, 146
   growth, 133
   history, 26-28
   interest in Latin American news, 81, 100-103, 118
   market research, 39-40, 47, 51, 134
   measurement of, 50-54
   median income, 39, 47, 54, 67
   middle class, 67, 131, 132-133
   national advertising to, 41-42
   national composition, 81, 84
   national differences ignored in marketing, 49-50
   seen as both unique and part of U.S. general market, 48, 54-55
   similarity to general population, 43

About the Author

América Rodriguez, formerly a correspondent for National Public Radio (NPR), is Associate Professor in the Departments of Radio-TV-Film and Journalism of the College of Communication at the University of Texas at Austin. She has published articles on the history and marketing of the Hispanic audience and on the Latino news media in *Critical Studies of Mass Communication, Quarterly Review of Film and Video, Communication Review,* and *Aztlán, A Journal of Chicano Studies,* as well as several mass communication anthologies. She received a B.A. in English and Spanish literature from Swarthmore College and an M.A. and Ph.D. in communication from the University of California at San Diego.